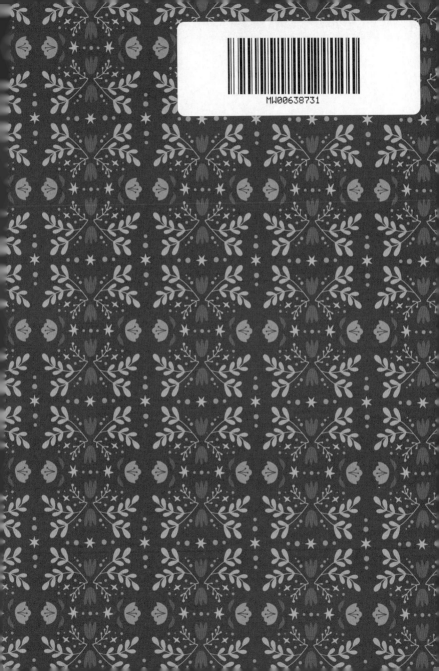

MW00638731

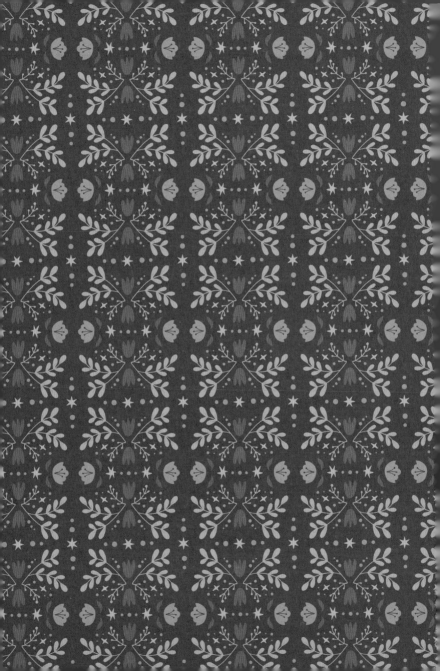

TO

_____

FROM

_____

DATE

_____

To my son, Scott.
You are an amazing young man—
handcrafted by God and a treasure to us both!

Mum

PURE
JOY

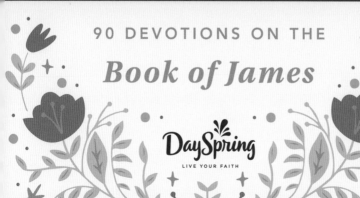

90 DEVOTIONS ON THE
Book of James

DaySpring
LIVE YOUR FAITH

Pure Joy: 90 Devotions on the Book of James
Copyright © 2024 DaySpring. All rights reserved.
First Edition, January 2024

Published by:

21154 Highway 16 East
Siloam Springs, AR 72761
dayspring.com

Written by: Anita Higman
Cover Design by: Hannah Brinson

Printed in China
Prime: J9613
ISBN: 978-1-64870-933-3

CONTENTS

INTRODUCTION

Life is broken.

We keep trying and trying—and trying—to make something worthwhile out of life, but no matter what we do on our own, it's still a hopelessly shattered mess. When we allow Christ to love His way into our lives, we discover this miraculous thing called grace. He can take what is broken by wrongdoing and refashion it into a magnificent work of art. And He gives us a new lightness of heart and a livelier step. Best of all, Paradise has been regained! Yes, that is us—when we journey humbly with Him.

It has been said that some of James's inspired writings have similarities to the book of Proverbs. So, I am hopeful you will also enjoy *Pausing for Proverbs*—the little inset devotions that are folded into this work.

May these ninety devotions and your journey with James flood your life with hope, ripen your faith, and transform you into a woman who knows how to dance in God's light and His wonderful ways of joy…

Anita Higman

BEYOND OUR IMAGININGS

James, a servant of God and of the Lord Jesus Christ,
to the twelve tribes scattered among the nations:
Greetings.

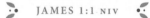 JAMES 1:1 NIV

Have you ever had anybody wave at you frantically and scream, "You're going the wrong way!" It's mortifying, especially when you realize that you're driving full throttle, going the wrong way into oncoming traffic! Our earthly journey can be riddled with those kinds of jolts—as well as a thousand other kinds.

We've all been there. We're going down a path that we feel makes the most sense, all our friends are going the same way, but something just doesn't seem right. And you wonder what God thinks about it. Could He be saying, "My friend, you're headed in the wrong direction"? When Jesus came to us, He did not burst onto the scene as a mighty reigning king—that glorious event will come later—but He arrived as a baby who became a humble servant as well as a friend and Redeemer. Not really what mankind had hoped for at the time.

But His divine ways are hard for us to fathom. The book of Isaiah reads, *"'For My thoughts are not your thoughts, neither are your ways My ways,' declares the LORD"* (55:8 NIV).

In the opening verse provided, we read that James is calling himself a servant of God and of Christ. Secretly we may groan over the word servant because it sounds like the antithesis to fun. But a spirit of servanthood—that is, focusing on the needs of others as well as our own—is the attitude that will delight God and delight us. As we pour out our lives for Him and for others, we are filled with soul riches that are beyond our imaginings, both now and for all time. And remember, the Word of God also says, *"Humble yourselves, therefore, under the mighty hand of God so that at the proper time he may exalt you"* (1 Peter 5:6 ESV).

How beautiful is that?

O Lord, my God, keep me from going full throttle
the wrong way in this life. It will surely lead to calamity.
Let me see heaven's way in all things. Amen.

A QUEST FOR
REAL JOY

Count it all joy, my brothers,
when you meet trials of various kinds, for you know
that the testing of your faith produces steadfastness.
And let steadfastness have its full effect, that you may be
perfect and complete, lacking in nothing.

 JAMES 1:2–4 ESV

Everybody's definition of *joy* is different. Some folks might light up in ecstasy as they take a zip line across a deep canyon. Others might instead throw up. Some people are elated when they speak in front of big audiences, while others consider this to be pure torture, so they, too, might throw up. Some individuals love eating chicken livers, and yet others—you guessed it.

Whatever your joys are, various earthly trials don't usually make it on that happy list. But Jesus told us clearly, *"I have said these things to you, that in me you may have peace. In the world you will have tribulation. But take heart; I have overcome the world"* (John 16:33 ESV).

The bottom line is that tribulation is a part of this broken life, but no one wants to line up for any of it. We want life to be purpose filled, chock-full of much love and many good things. A family, a nice home, and a good job. God sees these elements of life as joys, too, but He also wants us to know that trials can be counted as joy if we lean into Him and make full use of these trials for our growth and His glory.

Oh, yay. More of that painful, spiritual stuff. And yet many times, the people who have truly wowed us and challenged us and inspired us over the years were the people who have been through the deeper trials of this life. They gained some serious maturity—a divine steadfastness—and the miracle of it illuminated their lives. And ours.

What difficulties are we going through today that can be used as God's wow factor in the future? To change us? To change the world?

Lord, help me to find a way not only to accept
adversities that come my way, but even to count them
for joy, knowing You will find a way to make me more
like You in the process. Amen.

WHO CAN FATHOM!

If any of you lacks wisdom, let him ask God,
who gives generously to all without reproach,
and it will be given him.

> JAMES 1:5 ESV

Wisdom almost seems to have an unreachable quality to it, doesn't it? So, how do we even know when we possess this attribute? Well, wisdom might be easier to understand when we look at the opposite of wisdom—foolishness. Some people act foolishly because they lack knowledge, and yet they charge forward relentlessly, driven by their unwavering confidence in their instincts. While it's easy for us to say "we'd never do that," if we're honest with ourselves, we'd probably admit that we've found ourselves making foolish choices before.

Okay, so how does one acquire this valuable character trait called wisdom? Amazingly, God says to just ask for it. Really? Just like that? Yes, and He'll give wisdom to us generously. A fine example of this is when King Solomon—even as a boy—asked for wisdom, and God was very pleased to be asked.

"Give me an understanding heart so that I can govern Your people well and know the difference between right and wrong. . . . So God replied, "Because you have asked for wisdom in governing My people with justice and have not asked for a long life or wealth or the death of your enemies—I will give you what you asked for! I will give you a wise and understanding heart such as no one else has had or ever will have! And I will also give you what you did not ask for—riches and fame!" (I Kings 3:9–13 NLT)

This seems so excessively, wonderfully over the top, and yet—who can fathom the generosity of God?

Lord, I love it that You are such a lavish Giver.
I do desire Your divine wisdom in all things. Amen.

A CHEERFUL MIND WORKS HEALING

A happy heart is good medicine and a cheerful mind works healing, but a broken spirit dries up the bones.

 PROVERBS 17:22 AMPC

With the breathless whirl of ever-changing global events, well, many would say that a happy heart and a cheerful mind are a little hard to come by, and yet we need this mindset to face whatever the world brings our way. So, how can we possess these good things written about in Proverbs?

In the book of Matthew, we are reminded to keep our eyes on Christ: *"But immediately Jesus spoke to them, saying, 'Take heart; it is I. Do not be afraid.' And Peter answered him, 'Lord, if it is you, command me to come to you on the water.' He said, 'Come.' So Peter got out of the boat and walked on the water and came to Jesus. But when he saw the wind, he was afraid, and beginning to sink he cried out, 'Lord, save me.' Jesus immediately reached out his hand and took hold of* him, saying to him, 'O you of little faith, why did you doubt?'" (14:27–31 ESV).

May we keep our eyes on Jesus, whether the seas are silvery still or raging all around us. Jesus says not to be afraid. We are to keep the faith! But if we do falter, Jesus is always ready to lovingly reach His hand down to us, just as He did with Peter. Grab hold!

Dear Jesus, when I wake in the night,
my mind keeps mulling over all my problems.
May my fear be replaced with an unwavering faith
in You, and yes, may that deep trust keep me filled
with peace and joy. Amen.

FAMILY FOR
ALL TIME

If you don't know what you're doing, pray to the Father.
He loves to help. You'll get His help, and won't be
condescended to when you ask for it. Ask boldly,
believingly, without a second thought. People who
"worry their prayers" are like wind-whipped waves.
Don't think you're going to get anything from the Master
that way, adrift at sea, keeping all your options open.

JAMES 1:5–8 THE MESSAGE

When you want something from your spouse, your parents, your friend—how do you ask for it? Do you feel comfortable enough in your relationship to ask boldly, without holding back? Maybe you ask in one breath, and then take it back in the next. Or maybe you give hints, hoping they will guess. In James 1:5–8, we are told to boldly ask God for what we need and to truly believe that He will help us.

Here is one example in God's Word about going to Him audaciously and asking for what we need: *"Then Jesus said to them, 'Suppose you have a friend, and you go to him at midnight and say, "Friend, lend me three loaves of bread; a friend of mine on a journey has come to me, and I have no food to offer him." And suppose the one inside answers, "Don't bother me. The door is already locked, and my children and I are in bed. I can't get up and give you anything." I tell you, . . . because of your shameless audacity he will surely get up and give you as much as you need"'* (Luke 11:5–8 NIV).

So, it's okay to ask God for something again and again? Yes. Can we even plead our case and wrestle with Him? Yes, of course. Our boldness shows the Lord that we take Him seriously. And it shows us that we are not living an anemic sort of Christian half-life, but we are smackdab in the middle of a larger-than-life, love-infused relationship with Jesus Christ! Not a fleeting affair of the heart. No, we are family—for all time.

Oh, Jesus, I am so profoundly grateful to You that I can talk to You, sharing all my heart and soul. When I make my requests, please help me to ask boldly without doubting. Amen.

A DAILY DOSE
OF HUMILITY

Everyone proud and arrogant in heart is disgusting,
hateful, and exceedingly offensive to the Lord;
be assured [I pledge it] they will not go unpunished.

PROVERBS 16:5 AMPC

Pride is as old as time, and it is what still gets us into trouble today. We have heard enough proverbs on pride that one might think we'd know better. But many times, we still embrace smugness like it's an old friend.

Pride and arrogance are deceptive companions that can subtly infiltrate our thoughts, attitudes, and actions. They puff us up with self-importance, blinding us to our dependence on God and fostering an unhealthy sense of superiority. We begin to view ourselves as the center of the universe, disregarding the inherent worth and dignity of others.

It's always wise to remember that God does not take kindly to arrogance. In fact, He calls it disgusting and hateful and exceedingly offensive! And when we come across arrogance, we are disgusted too. It might help us to acknowledge the fact that haughtiness gains us nothing but unhappiness. It is far off the journey to real joy, and it certainly does not bring delight to our Lord. Maybe a spoonful of humility is in order, eh?

Dear God, give me a daily dose of humility, even when I don't like the taste of it. I really do want to please You in all my comings and goings. In Jesus's holy name I pray. Amen.

A BIG,
BEAUTIFUL LIFE

*Let the lowly brother boast in his exaltation,
and the rich in his humiliation, because like a flower
of the grass he will pass away. For the sun rises with its
scorching heat and withers the grass; its flower falls,
and its beauty perishes. So also will the rich man
fade away in the midst of his pursuits.*

> JAMES 1:9–11 ESV

When we arrive at a party, we tend to gravitate to the most with-it-looking person there—someone who might possess money, cleverness, or power. That is, someone who can improve our own circumstances in some way, perhaps even financially.

Everybody has done this social twiddling. Even at church! Well, money is useful, nice, and good. It is only the *love* of money that gets us into trouble. But boy, oh boy, it is so natural for us to romance the idea that money is the great buffer. The finest way to live a larger, more beautiful life. Hmmm.

So, how on earth are we to view wealth or the lack of it? Well, if you don't have a lot of money to speak of, you are being exalted in this life. If you are rich, know that there is an element of humiliation to it, because it can fade away as quickly as a flower wilting in the summer heat. The accumulation of wealth can become an obsession, as we desire it more and more. There can be an element of haughtiness, too, that slips in ever-so-slyly, as we come to feel we deserve it all.

But how does God's vantage point on wealth play out in day-to-day living? Well, it is right to enjoy and be thankful for the money God has given us, and not to be tightfisted, but instead openhanded with others who are in need. Yes, to glorify God with all we possess. Realistically, this balancing act sounds complicated and impossible in our humanness. It is, actually, but with God, all things are possible...

Dear Jesus, sometimes I have extra money and sometimes I don't. Please remind me of the way You see life here. That to You, a big, beautiful life is first having a humble spirit and enjoying the richness of Your divine presence. Amen.

A DRAMATIC DIFFERENCE

Pleasant words are as a honeycomb,
sweet to the mind and healing to the body.

 PROVERBS 16:24 AMPC

Many times, when you ask people what they want out of life, they reply that they'd like to make a real difference in this world. It is heartening to know that we are capable of accomplishing that feat every single day. Simply by the words we choose.

Do we select our words as carefully as we pick the sweet, ripe fruits at the market? Yes, we gaze at those peaches, gingerly squeeze them, as well as take in the fragrance of them to make sure they will bring maximum pleasure to our family and guests. If we decide to use that high level of care for merely picking fruit, could we not take even more care with the words we select to offer people? After all, words can injure folks for a lifetime, or they can uplift, challenge, encourage, and launch them into their God-given destiny.

The book of Proverbs also says, *"God can't stand evil scheming, but He puts words of grace and beauty on display"* (15:26 The Message).

How do our words come off? Pleasant as a honeycomb, and sweet to the mind as well as healing to the body? Are they full of grace and beauty? Will God want to put them on display? We can, indeed, make a dramatic difference in this world. With the power of our words...

Jesus, I often spew words just to fill the empty air.
Please give me pause before I speak,
and may my choice of words not be full of folly,
but wisdom. Amen.

FALLING IN LOVE WITH GOD

Anyone who meets a testing challenge head-on
and manages to stick it out is mighty fortunate.
For such persons loyally in love with God,
the reward is life and more life.

JAMES 1:12 THE MESSAGE

To be in love with God—what could those words really mean? God is, without a doubt, in love with us. Wouldn't we want to be in love with Him too? After all that He's done for us?

But even when we've embraced Christ as Friend and Redeemer, how does one actually go about loving Him? Is it easy or complex? Is it awesome or a bit scary? We know how to love a spouse, a child, and our friends. But what does this love for our God actually look like? Feel like? These are questions worth chasing. Maybe this miraculous process starts as a divine stirring deep in one's soul, as we curiously crave to know our Lord better, deeper. Then when we spend enough time in His presence, we begin to hear His loving, challenging, inspiring, illuminating, forgiving whispers and feel some of that profound peace we are promised in His Word. And also, in this ongoing creative, incandescent, and irresistible presence of our Lord, well, love happens.

Other ways we can love God is by enduring trials with patience, not giving in to temptations, and being obedient in what He asks us to do. Jesus told us, *"Those who accept My commandments and obey them are the ones who love Me. And because they love Me, My Father will love them. And I will love them and reveal Myself to each of them"* (John 14:21 NLT).

And so, what comes from all this mutual love with our Lord Jesus? Well, we will be blessed, and in the book of John, Christ promises to reveal Himself to us. And oh my, in those intimate moments with our Savior— joy arrives.

Dear God, I am in awe of who You are.
I want to learn to love You the way You deserve
to be loved. Show me how. Not because I want to earn
my way to heaven, but in grateful response to
Your offering of grace, mercy, and forgiveness!
In Jesus's name I pray. Amen.

TO SEE THE FACE OF CHRIST

There's a way that looks harmless enough;
look again—it leads straight to hell.

PROVERBS 16:25 THE MESSAGE

S ometimes in life we might find a road that looks pleasant enough. The road is paved and easy. There are lots of talkative people on that road, so you have plenty of company, even if the company gives you the spiritual shivers sometimes. Occasionally, you sense you might not be going the right way, and yet you figure that all the people marching forward—ever onward—must be right.

Besides, if you tried to turn back now, wouldn't everyone try to dissuade you anyway? They might make fun of you if you did choose to seek that other way again. Maybe they would do a lot worse than jeer at you. Then the devil whispers to you that you should stay put, even if you sense that ever-present and exalted road nearby, and you hear that splendid calling above the dark murmurings.

Then suddenly you heed that sweet and sacred summons, and you turn back. The soul-peace that had eluded you for a season, returns. Yes, there it is—Christ's way, His joy—real and ever-flowing...

Lord, I have known You as my Savior and Friend
for a while now, but lately I sense I have veered off from
Your path some. Please bring me back to You.
May I no longer keep straying from You,
but instead move ever closer to You. Amen.

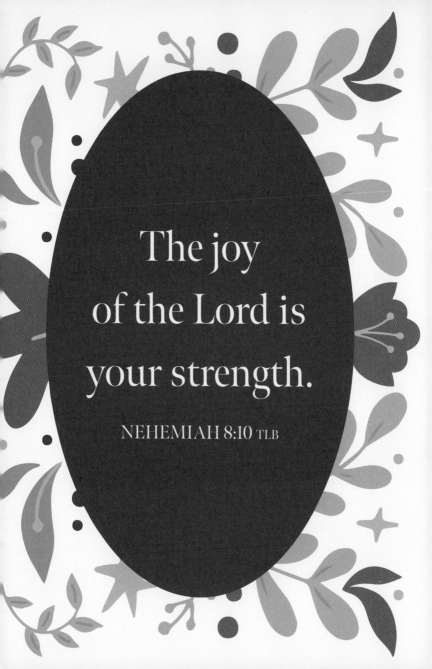

The joy
of the Lord is
your strength.

NEHEMIAH 8:10 TLB

OWNING UP

*Let no one say when he is tempted, "I am being
tempted by God," for God cannot be tempted with evil,
and he himself tempts no one. But each person is
tempted when he is lured and enticed by his own desire.
Then desire when it has conceived gives birth to sin,
and sin when it is fully grown brings forth death.*

JAMES 1:13–15 ESV

When Mom pops into the playroom to see why
things are getting dangerously quiet, well,
sometimes there is trouble. Maybe there's a broken toy,
a munched-up sack of cookies, or some other kind of
merry mischief. But even before Mom can raise a brow,
one child will invariably say, "She did it." Or, "It was
his idea!"

These kinds of scenarios among kids or adults are
as common as rain and as old as the Garden of Eden.
That is, pointing at someone else when it comes to our
own wrongdoing. We can read about the same spiritual
conundrum in the opening chapters of the Bible: *"He
[Adam] said, 'I heard You in the garden and I was afraid
because I was naked. And I hid.' GOD said, 'Who told*

you that you were naked? Did you eat from that tree I told you not to eat from?' The Man said, 'The Woman You gave me as a companion, she gave me fruit from the tree, and, yes, I ate it.' GOD said to the Woman, 'What is this that you've done?' 'The serpent seduced me,' she said, 'and I ate'" (Genesis 3:10–13 THE MESSAGE).

Okay, so Adam blamed Eve, and Eve blamed the serpent. So, at whom do we point our own fingers? Do we sometimes blame God for our sin or the consequences of it? For as it says in James, God does not tempt us. But the good news is that we can confess to the Lord, and forgiveness is both free and freeing! In addition, we can change with the power of the Holy Spirit. What a promise we see in the book of Titus: *"He saved us, not because of works done by us in righteousness, but according to his own mercy, by the washing of regeneration and renewal of the Holy Spirit"* (3:5 ESV).

A promise, indeed!

Jesus, I confess that I have sinned.
Please forgive me and help me to flee from the sin.
Amen.

A NOBLER WAY

Better to be patient than powerful; better to have self-control than to conquer a city.

PROVERBS 16:32 NLT

Humans are notorious for getting addicted to just about anything, and they can be pretty intense about it!

For instance, there is the compulsion to gain power. Once a person gets a taste for control, it can be really hard to give up. One might immediately think of the political world, but power over others can come in many forms. What if we manage to gain some serious dominance over those around us—those who might be younger, or more disadvantaged or poorer or older, or perhaps still in the womb? Power does tend to corrupt, and it may entice us to gain even more power. So, what happens if we allow that newly established authority over others to become abusive? It is not going to end well.

What other ways might we be flailing around spiritually or perhaps lacking in self-control? Has the enemy of our soul managed to get us to dance to his tunes? The current trends are saying that there is freedom in doing whatever we please. But the way of heaven is the opposite—better to be patient than powerful, and self-control is more honorable than conquering a city. God's way won't trap us on some kind of surreal spiritual carnival ride or an addictive treadmill, but it will free us to experience real peace and joy!

Lord, I don't want to be addicted to anything.
May I instead have patience and self-control in all I do.
Amen.

THE FATHER OF LIGHT

So, my very dear friends, don't get thrown off course. Every desirable and beneficial gift comes out of heaven. The gifts are rivers of light cascading down from the Father of Light. There is nothing deceitful in God, nothing two-faced, nothing fickle. He brought us to life using the true Word, showing us off as the crown of all His creatures.

JAMES 1:16–18 THE MESSAGE

Have you ever had a friend who changed like the wind or a shifting shadow? She might have told you she couldn't wait to see you again, but then she never called you up. Or a friend might have stated her case empathically on a vital issue, but then the next time you saw her, she said the opposite. Or perhaps someone dear to you enticed you with the promise of something wonderful, but it never happened. All these kinds of behaviors can make for irritating and exhausting relationships. Yes, people can be monstrously fickle!

But oh, we can, indeed, celebrate the fact that our friendship with God is not like that. When God promises us something in His Word, we can be assured that He will follow through. And so, when we see this crazy life falling apart, God is our comfort and our rock. He's not going anywhere! Trust Him. Lean on Him. God is, indeed, all these magnificent things mentioned in James. First Chronicles also happily proclaims to us, *"Oh, give thanks to the Lord, for He is good; His love and His kindness go on forever"* (16:34 TLB).

Yes, God is good and perfect and constant. Even when the pledges and assurances of friends, coworkers, relatives, and strangers fall flat, God is there, ever-present in good times and in times of trouble. Even when the human race turns away from the Lord's light and life, love and truth, we can take refuge in Him and embrace all the good things that come from His dear hand...

O God, I am so grateful You are right here with me, every minute of every day. I can always run to You, for You are always here wanting to help me. You alone are worthy of my trust! Amen.

BUILDING A GOOD LIFE

*A meal of bread and water in contented peace
is better than a banquet spiced with quarrels.*

 PROVERBS 17:1 THE MESSAGE

Have you ever seen someone steamroll into a room like they were ready to pick a fight? We have all been in that volatile firecracker mode, but there is a better way to live. Basically the book of Proverbs says that it is better to enjoy simple foods in peace than to sit at a feast where people are arguing up a storm.

If we always go around with a short fuse, our Christian walk is going to get unnecessarily rough, and the light of Christ that we are called to radiate onto a darkened world cannot shine as brightly. When we do get into a quarrel, then what? Ephesians encourages us with this: *"If you are angry, don't sin by nursing your grudge. Don't let the sun go down with you still angry—get over it quickly; for when you are angry, you give a mighty foothold to the devil"* (4:26–27 TLB).

May we not give the devil a foothold by holding on to our anger. Do we need to pray some more about the situation? Do we need to apologize or forgive or reconcile with someone? Afterward, we will be able to breathe easier, eat better, and sleep more deeply. Ahhh.

May we not spice up our conversations with barbs and prickles and peevishness, but with wisdom, compassion, and an unassuming nature. Yes, with honesty, encouragement, and love. Indeed, these are beautiful blocks to assemble a good and joy-filled life.

Lord, I get angry too easily and too often.
Please give my soul an overhaul in this area of my life.
Amen.

A FINER PLACE
TO LIVE

Know this, my beloved brothers:
let every person be quick to hear, slow to speak,
slow to anger.

>• JAMES 1:19 ESV •<

E ver met anyone who… Never. Stops. Talking?

Oy! You want to slap your head or cause a distraction or become invisible. Yeah, those people can really stick out at a party or at the office or in line at the coffee shop or during church or anywhere really. Talk becomes their chief commodity, and they peddle an abundance of it everywhere they go. Common sense might say that to listen is to learn. Instead, they gab, chew the fat, repeat stories, and pontificate on all topics and yet appear to possess little knowledge, wisdom, or even courtesy.

Also, too much talk can get us into trouble. When we become a motormouth, just the sheer volume of yak that gushes like a fire hose, can almost guarantee that the yak will eventually offend, morph into gossip, or at the least, make us look like egotistical clowns. Oh my. The book of James says to be quick to hear others while turning down our own spigot. And Proverbs tells us plainly, *"Even a fool who keeps silent is considered wise; when he closes his lips, he is deemed intelligent"* (17:28 ESV).

God is trying to help us with this pesky human tendency that gets in our way and in the way of others. But how does one truly implement this temperance of the tongue when we love to hear ourselves talk? The Holy Spirit can show us when to listen and when to speak and give us the power to overcome these compulsions to chatter away. And our lives—as well as the world—will become a finer place to live…

God, I admit I often talk too much wherever I go. Please help me to know when to listen and when to speak. I need not only guidance, but the daily discipline to follow through with Your directions. Amen.

MORE ALIVE
THAN EVER

Understand [this], my beloved brethren.
Let every man be quick to hear [a ready listener],
slow to speak, slow to take offense and to get angry.

JAMES 1:19 AMPC

Yes, James brings up some common human frailties here, and this devotion will deal with the last segment of the verse, which is just as indispensable as the first part! Anger—that topic isn't fun to talk about. But everybody who's still breathing is surely dealing with it. Maybe every single day.

To feel the emotion of anger is not always a sin, but it can certainly lead to sin. If it is not dealt with God's way, then the devil can get some traction in our lives, and it can lead to unforgiveness, bitterness, grudges, or revenge. We can't avoid all anger in this life. Even Jesus became angry when confronted with the moneychangers who were desecrating the Temple—and Jesus never once sinned. But wouldn't it be freeing to know how to deal with our anger? Ephesians says, "*BE ANGRY [at sin—at immorality, at injustice, at ungodly behavior], YET DO*

NOT SIN; do not let your anger [cause you shame, nor allow it to] last until the sun goes down. And do not give the devil an opportunity [to lead you into sin by holding a grudge, or nurturing anger, or harboring resentment, or cultivating bitterness]" (4:26–27 AMP).

These verses in Ephesians don't give us carte blanche when it comes to anger but acknowledge that there can be valid reasons for these emotions. For instance, all kinds of injustices and immoral behavior can cause us righteous indignation, which is understandable. Sometimes the anger is connected to our own sinful behaviors. Yikes! However, when the emotion does arrive, the keys to dealing with it are to be slow to anger. And not to allow the sun to go down before we have dealt with it the right way, whether through prayer or an apology or whatever God asks of us.

No matter where the anger comes from, dealing with it in a godly fashion will help us to face each new day, fresh and free, and more alive than ever!

Lord, when I get angry in this life,
help me to deal with it properly. Amen.

A BOUNTIFUL EYE

He who is generous will be blessed,
for he gives some of his food to the poor.

PROVERBS 22:9 AMP

Have you ever been in a situation where you could not make ends meet? You were living from paycheck to paycheck, and you knew that if anything went wrong, you would find yourself in terrible debt? And then it happened. The unthinkable. You had an accident, and you ended up with a bill that could not be fully paid. How would God take care of you now?

Then out of the blue, someone came in and helped you. The tears of joy fell like sweet rain, and you were never the same again. Something deep in your soul was stirred, and once you were on your feet again, you found a way to help others in the same way.

And so, the tender mercies rippled on. God loves it when we are generous with others. When we have offered food or finances or a cup of cool water, we have entered into what might be called a sacred space—a place where God finds delight.

How can we bless others today, and in so doing, bring joy to the heart of God?

Mighty God, I have been so awed by Your care for me. Sometimes You work these sweet miracles through Your followers, and I thank You for the many ways You bless us. May I always remember to care for others in the same way. Give me a bountiful eye! In Jesus's powerful name I pray. Amen.

TAKES
THE PRESSURE
RIGHT OFF!

For the [resentful, deep-seated] anger of man
does not produce the righteousness of God
[that standard of behavior which He requires from us].

JAMES 1:20 AMP

As we read today's verse, we might suddenly get tripped up on the concept of righteousness. In all candor, it is a spiritual ideal that trips us all up, whether we are dealing with anger or any number of other issues. One way to describe righteousness is "being in right standing with God." But no matter how hard we try, "self" just keeps getting in our way!

In fact, have you ever met anyone who dripped with self-righteousness? Jesus is not big on the smuggishness of a "self" mindset. He told us in this parable, *"Two men went up into the temple to pray, one a Pharisee and the other a tax collector. The Pharisee, standing by himself, prayed thus: 'God, I thank you that I am not like* other men, extortioners, unjust, adulterers, or even like this tax collector. I fast twice a week; I give tithes of all that I get.' But the tax collector, standing far off, would not even lift up his eyes to heaven, but beat his breast, saying, 'God, be merciful to me, a sinner!' I tell you, this man went down to his house justified, rather than the other. For everyone who exalts himself will be humbled, but the one who humbles himself will be exalted" (Luke 18:10–14 ESV).

Then, how are we to do this real and righteous and impossible thing for the Lord?

When Jesus asks us to be righteous, He doesn't mean for us to be fueled by "self." He wants us to be propelled with His supernatural power—not ours. Big difference. What a relief, actually, since it takes the pressure right off us. One can feel the weariness of the endless striving just melt away. Ahhhhh.

Lord, thank You that I don't have to rely on my own grit to do life, but that I can do all things through You. Amen.

GOD HAS THE LAST SAY

Do not fret because of evildoers or be envious of the wicked, for the evildoer has no future hope, and the lamp of the wicked will be snuffed out.

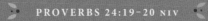

PROVERBS 24:19–20 NIV

People can safely say that our world has known great travails. Sorrows of many kinds have visited our homes, there are weekly reports that appear catastrophic in nature, and our futures seem fraught with even more fears. Not just worries of the unknown, but deep concerns over what are real threats to us and our world. At times, it feels too much to comprehend and too much to handle.

May we always keep in mind that God gets the last say in this world. God is still on the throne, and His plan will ultimately prevail. In the end, God wins, and so do all those who love and follow Him.

Isn't it calming and hopeful to remember these words of our Savior: *"In My Father's house there are many dwelling places (homes). If it were not so, I would have told you; for I am going away to prepare a place for you"* (John 14:2 AMPC). Oh yes, heaven awaits those who follow Christ, our Lord. What joy sublime!

*Lord, I am so glad that You have prepared a place
for me in heaven and that You are coming back.
I love You with all my heart and soul. Amen.*

A LIFE
WELL LIVED!

*So walk out on your corrupt liaison with smut
and depraved living, and humbly welcome the word
of truth that will blossom like the seed of
salvation planted in your souls.*

>• JAMES 1:21 THE VOICE •<

James—whom many believe is Jesus's half-brother—
does not mince words. He gives it to us straight. There
is no putting a pretty spin on the sadness in our world
today. The good news is that we can step away from
it all. We don't need to spin with the rest of the earth.
We can whirl with God instead and discover plenty of
happiness with Him until His Son returns for us.

Yes, we can walk away from what is cruel and instead
step closer to God and all His glories. His beauty,
creativity, and compassion. His hope-filled and forgiving
ways. His presence, His purposes for us, His healing
touch, and miracles, mercy, and goodness. Oh, and His
forever love that enfolds us, challenges us, protects us,
comforts us, and gives us the power to spiritually grow
and flourish!

Ahhh, yes—a life well lived, rich and real. James would like that.

So, there is no need to despair. The Lord is here in our midst. Let's join Him!

Jesus, I love You. I admit I have suffered with a fear of the future. Please help me always to remember that You give me the power to step away from whatever is trying to invade my life. Help me to embrace all the hope You offer and to know that You are with me every minute of every day. Amen.

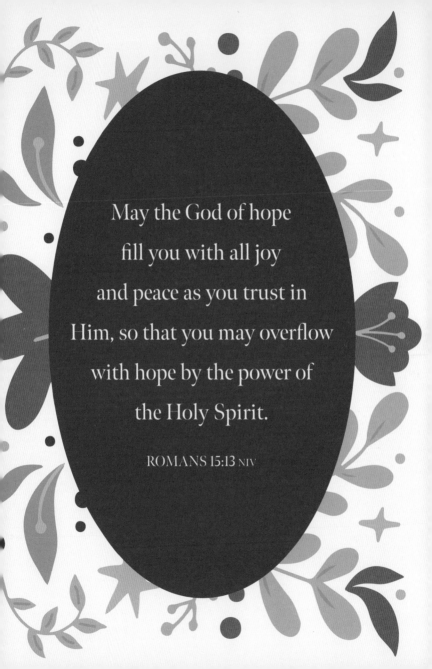

May the God of hope
fill you with all joy
and peace as you trust in
Him, so that you may overflow
with hope by the power of
the Holy Spirit.

ROMANS 15:13 NIV

WHAT WILL THE LORD SAY?

All the ways of a man are clean and innocent in his own eyes [and he may see nothing wrong with his actions], But the LORD weighs and examines the motives and intents [of the heart and knows the truth].

PROVERBS 16:2 AMP

Have you ever noticed that when two friends have a falling-out, there are usually two distinctly different stories told as to what led to the severing of their friendship? Usually it plays out like this—you feel that you have been wronged monstrously, and you have a long and detailed list as to how that is absolute truth. So, how does the other friend feel about the same situation? Well, that friend feels she was horribly wronged, and she also has a long and detailed list of how her side of the story is the unquestionable truth. Oh dear. Now what?

Yes, some people really do wrong us, and sometimes they do it with ill intent, and they do it epically. But many times, we are also at fault, and acknowledging our sin in the matter is a hard thing to do.

According to Proverbs, we may need a second look at our motivations and intents of the heart. Whether we are talking about relationships or anything else, we usually can't claim total innocence.

What will the Lord say about us when He examines our motives today?

Lord, I have fallen out with someone we both know,
and well, I am not sure what went wrong.
Help me to know if it is my fault
and what I can do to make it right. Amen.

WE HAVE ALL
BEEN THERE

*Don't fool yourself into thinking that you are a listener
when you are anything but, letting the Word go in one
ear and out the other. Act on what you hear!
Those who hear and don't act are like those who glance
in the mirror, walk away, and two minutes later have
no idea who they are, what they look like.*

> JAMES 1:22–24 THE MESSAGE

If you're a mom, you know that sometimes when you
hear a verbal skirmish going on with the kids, you
do your best to impersonate a brilliant counselor. You
tell your kids how fabulously they were created by God
but that they're not acting like it at the moment. You
might make firm suggestions for improvement or take
away privileges if it was a major offense. The kiddos do
their usual nodding routine and make you think they
will, indeed, do better next time. So, feeling good about
your parenting skills, you head back to the kitchen to
make dinner. And, of course, the siblings immediately
begin to thump and thrash on each other with renewed

gusto. So, you stand there, dumfounded and thinking, *Well, good grief. What is that?*

What is that, indeed? Perhaps a disinterest in obeying? Is that how we sometimes act with God? The Lord might advise us in our quiet times, or we might get divine guidance in the Bible, or perhaps we will hear good counsel in a sermon, but the minute we get immersed back in our daily lives, we immediately do the opposite of what we know is right.

Sigh. Yeah, we have all been there.

Acknowledging the problem and relying on God to change us is a positive first step. With His help, we can, without a doubt, be doers of the Word! People want to be wowed by our walk with God. They want to know that the Lord makes a difference not only in what we say, but also in what we actually do. And our enduring authenticity—coupled with God's power—can, indeed, change the world...

Lord, please let me be a doer of Your Word. Amen.

IT MADE ALL THE DIFFERENCE

Do not withhold good from those to whom it is due,
when it is in your power to do it.

 PROVERBS 3:27 ESV

Have you ever felt so tired emotionally and spiritually it was like you were running on fumes? You began to crave a kind word or a piece of caring advice or a genuine word of encouragement. And then, when that smile and support arrived, you nearly burst into tears of joy?

We have all felt needy in one way or another. Perhaps you or someone you know needs a bit of help with the kids or a homemade casserole or a listening ear. This type of list can go on and on.

If people we know are truly in need, and if we are able to help or offer a kind word, may we consider extending that good thing to them whatever it is. Sometimes our thoughtfulness can mean the difference between someone spiraling into despair or seeing hope and possibilities and a new way to go. That can be us.

Yes, we can be the ones to inspire a song in someone's heart and make a burden lighter.

May the Lord one day say of us, "Yes, she did not withhold the good, and what she did made all the difference." Let it be so...

Dear Jesus, if there is someone whom I need to help today, please bring him or her to mind. Give me wisdom in this matter as well as courage and a generous spirit. Amen.

LIVING BY THE
BEAUTIFUL TRUTHS

But the one who looks into the perfect law,
the law of liberty, and perseveres,
being no hearer who forgets but a doer who acts,
he will be blessed in his doing.

JAMES 1:25 ESV

Have you ever promised to do something for someone and then forgot? You probably really intended to follow through, but things got really busy, and it just slipped your mind. It's never fun to realize you let someone down because you didn't do your part.

Jesus appreciates our follow-through, and He reminds us of this basic concept when He said, *"'What do you think? A man had two sons. And he went to the first and said, "Son, go and work in the vineyard today." And he answered, "I will not," but afterward he changed his mind and went. And he went to the other son and said the same. And he answered, "I go, sir," but did not go. Which of the two did the will of his father?' They said, 'The first.' Jesus said to them, 'Truly, I say to you, the tax* collectors and the prostitutes go into the kingdom of God before you'" (Matthew 21:28–31 ESV).

So, to live—really live and follow through with God's flawless and beautiful truths, day by day by day—well, we will know freedom and we will be blessed. One could call this sweet assurance in James a path to joy. And don't we all want more real joy?

Dear God, lately I have been lacking joy in my life.
To be honest, I don't feel all that free or blessed.
I wonder if I have strayed so far away from Your divine
precepts that it has caused me to suffer spiritually.
Please draw near to me and help me. Please allow Your
beautiful and flawless Word to seep deeply into my soul,
and may it change my life. May living all Your divine
truths day by day become my joy and Your delight.
In Jesus's powerful name I pray! Amen.

WHAT WILL PEOPLE SAY?

Above all else, watch over your heart;
diligently guard it because from a sincere and pure
heart come the good and noble things of life.

 **PROVERBS 4:23 THE VOICE**

When folks gather together someday to celebrate your life at your memorial service, what do you think they will say about you? Maybe that you lived life large and did it all your way? That you made it to the top of your class, your career, and you were victorious in reaching all your educational and financial dreams? There's nothing wrong with goals, but when those praises and accolades stand alone, won't they suddenly take on a shallow feel and fade away like a mist?

Perhaps instead of living mostly for ourselves, we could live Proverbs 4:23. Then they might say, "She was such a kindhearted woman, so generous—a woman of true substance. Much love surrounded her family, and oh, how she loved Jesus. She will be greatly missed here. But she will be welcomed in heaven!"

All our choices matter. Our lives matter. Our love matters. Most importantly, our redemption in Christ matters.

What will people say about us on that very last day?

Almighty God, I want to be remembered as a woman with a good and noble spirit who followed You and loved You with her whole heart all the days of her life. And then, on that fine and radiant day when I arrive in heaven, I will look forward to running into Your arms. In Jesus's magnificent name I pray. Amen.

IT WILL BE
PURE JOY!

*Anyone who says he is a Christian but doesn't control
his sharp tongue is just fooling himself,
and his religion isn't worth much.*

JAMES 1:26 TLB

We've all said things we wish we could take back.
Things that have caused emotional pain for
others. And while we may instantly feel bad for the words
that just left our mouths, we can't take them back. Words
can cause wounds that last for months or a lifetime.
Proverbs says, *"Words kill, words give life; they're either
poison or fruit—you choose"* (18:21 THE MESSAGE).

Wow, that verse is so clear and concise. Let's do that!
Won't the days of our lives be so much better if we all
follow that guidance? To choose life and not death with
our words—to choose fruit and not poison? Seems like
an easy choice, the satisfying choice, the only choice. But
when you get down to the street level and the nitty-gritty
of our hours on this earth—with problematic people and
circumstances that seem impossible—oh, how one can

dip into the poison talk and start wide-mouthing it with anything but sweet fruit.

The book of Romans has even more hard truths to say about our speech: *"Their throats are open graves; their tongues practice deceit. The poison of vipers is on their lips. Their mouths are full of cursing and bitterness"* (3:13–14 NIV).

So, how can we hand out sweet fruit with our lives instead of the rotten apples? If we are in constant communion with our Lord—and our souls are so powerfully and closely intertwined with Him—how would we then spew poison?

Sweet, intimate fellowship with Jesus equals sweet fruit pouring out from our lives. The whole world will taste the difference in us, and it will be pure joy.

Lord, may we stay in constant fellowship all day, remaining so close that poisonous words never even want to make it to my heart, let alone my lips. Amen.

WHAT IS WRITTEN ON OUR HEARTS

Don't lose your grip on Love and Loyalty.
Tie them around your neck; carve their initials
on your heart. Earn a reputation for living well
in God's eyes and the eyes of the people.

 PROVERBS 3:3–4 THE MESSAGE

When humans ponder love, they may not always link that feeling with loyalty. In fact, how many times do we all precariously dangle from the fragile tendrils of "feeling"? Not a safe or steady place to be. Our moods, no matter how passionate at the time, can be fleeting, and if love is linked merely to volatile emotions, our love can be transitory too.

God wants so much more for us than we want for ourselves and for others. Sometimes we grab after whatever is in easy reach—the cheaper, faster, imitation version of life—when God is offering the real deal. That is, what is beautiful and authentic and eternal. The Lord wants faithfulness as well as genuine love to be written on our hearts.

If we make these pure ideals an intimate part of our daily lives and we live well in the sight of God, won't pure joy surely follow?

Lord God, I need to remember that along with loving You and others, I also need loyalty. Help me to live well in Your eyes. And when people witness my love and steadfastness and joy, they may ask how I came by such blessings. They may then want to ask about You. Please let it be so! In Jesus's name I pray. Amen.

TAKING OURSELVES OFF THE SHELF

Religion that is pure and undefiled before
God the Father is this: to visit orphans and widows
in their affliction, and to keep oneself unstained
from the world.

JAMES 1:27 ESV

U h-oh—sounds like we're supposed to be doing more than just talking to God and talking *about* God in this life. James says we're supposed to be helping orphans and widows too. Hmmm. And the Bible talks a lot about kindness and compassion and helping those who are in need. At this point, most busy folks begin to think, *Hey, that sounds pretty good, but quite a time-consuming endeavor. Not sure I can commit to one more thing.* And others might add, "I thought we weren't saved by works, but we're saved by grace through faith in Christ!" Yes, that is true.

James is not teaching salvation by works, but don't we love God so dearly for what He has done for us in Christ that we would like to thank Him with good deeds? Our hearts say yes! And Ephesians reminds us, *"For by grace you have been saved through faith. And this is not your own doing; it is the gift of God, not a result of works, so that no one may boast. For we are his workmanship, created in Christ Jesus for good works, which God prepared beforehand, that we should walk in them"* (2:8–10 ESV).

So, yes, we are, indeed, saved by grace through faith in Christ. But it's easy to pass over the second part of this passage from Ephesians, which mentions the good works that God would like us to do—works, in fact, that He has actually prepared for us to do.

Is God calling us to take ourselves down off the shelf and get busy doing His good work? Yeah. He is. What would the Lord have you do today for His Kingdom? There is much to be done and joy to be had in it!

*Dear Jesus, I want Your work to be done,
and I want to be a part of it. Show me how to do
Your will until the day You take me home. When we're
face-to-face someday, I long for You to say to me,
"Well done, My good and faithful servant." Amen.*

CAREENING TOWARD PERIL

*The way of the [arrogant] fool [who rejects
God's wisdom] is right in his own eyes, but a wise
and prudent man is he who listens to counsel.*

PROVERBS 12:15 AMP

When you're at the movies, the audience always cringes when the hero or heroine is hurtling toward some horrific peril. It makes us want to shout out, "Don't do it! Don't go into that dark parking lot alone!" Or maybe, "You're driving right toward a cliff!" We may witness a wide variety of frightful moments in real life. A beloved friend or relative or acquaintance decides to do something extremely risky, and we, too, want to shout, "Stop!" And sometimes we *do* shout a little—because this isn't the movies, and the consequences can be scary and painful for everyone involved. In this life, foolishness is so prevalent and popular, it can chase us right into our nightmares. That is good reason to stay close to the Source of all life and wisdom—God.

Second Timothy reminds us that God is not hiding, nor is His wisdom: *"All Scripture is inspired by God and is useful to teach us what is true and to make us realize what is wrong in our lives. It corrects us when we are wrong and teaches us to do what is right"* (3:16 NLT).

If we, as lovers of Christ, stay connected to the Lord and His inspired Word—the Bible—we are on a road that leads not to ruin, but to joy.

Dear Lord, help me to seek Your wisdom in all areas of my life. Amen.

MORE OF YOU, LORD!

. . . keep oneself unstained from the world.

> JAMES 1:27 ESV

The second half to this verse in James may be brief, but it has enormous value! So, how can a person keep herself unstained by the world? How can we safeguard ourselves against negative influences and the complexities of the world? Although darkness may attempt to infiltrate our beings, let us remember that we possess the power to shine brightly, like radiant stars in the night sky.

The book of Romans has another profound verse about staying uncorrupted: *"Do not be conformed to this world, but be transformed by the renewal of your mind, that by testing you may discern what is the will of God, what is good and acceptable and perfect"* (12:2 ESV).

Hmmm. Interesting word—*conformed.* Since women love tablecloths, their properties might come to mind concerning that word. How satisfying when we lift a tablecloth out of the drawer, give it a few good shakes to flap out all the wrinkles, and then allow the cloth to float down onto whatever surface we're embellishing. If it is a wispy material in particular, the fabric will *conform* to whatever is underneath. Ahh, yes.

If Christ is the foundation for all we do—and all we are—then, like that silken cloth, we will naturally conform to Him and all His marvelous and beautiful and perfect ways. And that, my friend, will always be the most joyful way to live.

Dear God, please be the foundation of my life,
in all I do and all I say. May I always remain in You!
Thank You for watching over me and keeping me safe!
In Jesus's holy name I pray. Amen.

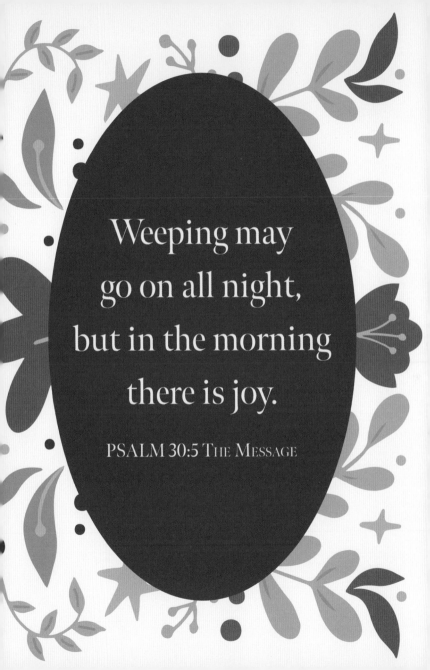

Weeping may
go on all night,
but in the morning
there is joy.

PSALM 30:5 THE MESSAGE

REAL FRIENDSHIP

*Faithful are the wounds of a friend
[who corrects out of love and concern],
but the kisses of an enemy are deceitful
[because they serve his hidden agenda].*

PROVERBS 27:6 AMP

We have all experienced the ebb and flow of friendships. They come and go all through our lives. Hopefully, we eventually learn how to choose friendships wisely. Sometimes those relationships reflect a myriad of emotions, and don't we just love it when our friends praise us and encourage and support us? It makes us feel safe and cozy and good, right?

But what happens if that friend reprimands us for something we're doing that might be questionable? Do we expect to be cheered on, no matter what? Even if we're caught doing something immoral or irresponsible?

That's where Proverbs comes in. Isn't it better for you to receive the rebuke of a friend—even if her timing or wording might not be perfect—rather than to relish the company of a person who keeps on praising you for no reason? If that latter individual is just flinging flattery with no thought of your well-being, then does she care about you? Maybe she is more of what might be referred to today as—well, a *frenemy*. Oh my.

What kind of friends have we chosen? And what kind of a friend are we to others? Aren't these good questions to bring up next time we talk to God? And isn't it wonderful that the Lord will never lie to us, but instead speak the truth in love!

Lord, help me to choose friends
who speak the truth in love. Amen.

WALKING HUMBLY WITH OUR GOD

*My fellow believers, do not practice your faith
in our glorious Lord Jesus Christ with an attitude
of partiality [toward people—show no favoritism,
no prejudice, no snobbery].*

 JAMES 2:1 AMP

In a busy world filled with division and discrimination, this passage in James serves as a gentle yet resolute reminder to rise above the tempting allure of favoritism and prejudice.

The book of Isaiah tells us, *"The haughty looks of man shall be brought low, and the lofty pride of men shall be humbled, and the Lord alone will be exalted in that day. For the Lord of hosts has a day against all that is proud and lofty, against all that is lifted up—and it shall be brought low"* (2:11–12 ESV).

Can there be any freedom from such galling behaviors like haughtiness and favoritism? The Holy Spirit can be a powerful help to us so that we can become more

Christlike every day. Wouldn't it be lovely to ask the Holy Spirit to show us the way of humility?

There are some exquisite words in Micah that speak of this: *"He has told you, O man, what is good; and what does the LORD require of you but to do justice, and to love kindness, and to walk humbly with your God?"* (6:8 ESV).

Walking humbly with our God. Ahhh. Such a more sanctified and lighter way to live. And when humility crowds out the haughtiness—there'll be more room for joy!

Holy Spirit, I want to let go of the burden of partiality.
I do it a lot, and sometimes automatically.
I need a new approach to life, one without snobbery.
And when I do slip into this kind of sin,
help me to repent and quickly make things right.
Thank You! Amen.

HASTE MAKES WASTE

Desire without knowledge is not good,
and to be overhasty is to sin and miss the mark.

 PROVERBS 19:2 AMPC

Have you ever been bent on a decision so intensely that there was nothing anyone could say to persuade you otherwise? Maybe your dear friend did try to caution or advise or implore you to take a different route, and maybe she even had Scriptures to back it up, but you refused because your desire was so strong. Then maybe days or months or years later, you wished you had listened to him or her, but it was too late.

Sometimes our impulsive desires and enthusiasms drive us to move at unnecessary speeds, and that wild haste causes us to miss the mark. How many countless times could our lives have been easier and happier if we had only prayed more or listened better?

Yes, desire sounds so wonderful, but without knowledge, the longing can go awry. Proverbs also says, *"People ruin their lives by their own foolishness and then are angry at the Lᴏʀᴅ"* (19:3 ɴʟᴛ). Yes, when life goes badly, the human response leans toward pointing our finger at someone else, and sometimes we end up blaming God.

There is only one real and wonderful way to live, and isn't it great that God wants to help us get there?

Dear Jesus, I am sorry for all the times
I have hastily made bad decisions. Please forgive me.
Show me how to slow down and become
a woman of wisdom. Amen.

POIGNANT REMINDER

If an affluent gentleman enters your gathering wearing
the finest clothes and priceless jewelry, don't trip over
each other trying to welcome him. And if a penniless
bum crawls in with his shabby clothes and a stench fills
the room, don't look away or pretend you didn't notice—
offer him a seat up front, next to you. If you tell the
wealthy man, "Come sit by me; there's plenty of room,"
but tell the vagrant, "Oh, these seats are saved.
Go over there," then you'll be judging
God's children out of evil motives.

JAMES 2:2–4 THE VOICE

Okay, in these potent verses in James, he takes his inspired speech a little further on the topic of favoritism. This tiny story is a poignant example of how we sometimes gush over those who can get us where we want to go in life while we ignore some people whom we think are below us in some way.

Perhaps we don't even realize we're acting this way, since it can come so naturally to us all. In fact, we might feel vindicated in our schmoozing, writing it off as networking. After all, doesn't everyone hang around with the right people to get ahead? You know, the powerful and wealthy players who can afford to invest in us, give us valuable advice, or help us in some way? It is surely rule-number-one if you want to move forward in your career. But building your business, developing valuable associates, and exchanging cards at a party is not the same thing as flattery and favoritism. The difference in the two will ultimately reside in our hearts, and God knows the difference very well in each of us—for He knows all our thoughts.

This verse in Psalms is powerful: *"May these words of my mouth and this meditation of my heart be pleasing in Your sight, Lord, my Rock and my Redeemer"* (19:14 NIV).

Yes, what a wise and wonderful life-verse to guide us each day.

Dear God, You know my every thought and all
my motivations, even better than I understand them.
Help me to please You in every area of my life.
May I be wise in all my dealings with people,
and may I always treat everyone the same,
knowing they are all precious in Your sight and all are
made in Your image. In Jesus's name I pray. Amen.

LORD, PLEASE HEAL OUR LAND!

When the righteous are in authority and become great,
the people rejoice; but when the wicked man rules,
the people groan and sigh.

PROVERBS 29:2 AMP

As a people, we need to always pray for good and righteous leaders. We were meant for Paradise, walking ever humbly with our God. But since the Fall of mankind, we have fallen further still, for we are not innocent. Can we ever turn things around? Can we ever see light in this landscape again?

Yes, indeed! In 2 Chronicles, the joyful news is clear: *"If My people, who are called by My name, will humble themselves and pray and seek My face and turn from their wicked ways, then I will hear from heaven, and I will forgive their sin and will heal their land"* (7:14 NIV).

Before the Lord returns, may we humble ourselves, pray, seek His face, and turn from our wicked ways.

Yes, indeed. May it be so!

Lord, bring us to a place of humility before You.
Please hear our prayers and heal our land.
We praise You. We worship and adore You,
for You are the King of kings and the Lord of lords!
Amen.

THE RIGHT END OF
THE KALEIDOSCOPE

*Listen to me, dear brothers and sisters. Hasn't God
chosen the poor in this world to be rich in faith?
Aren't they the ones who will inherit the Kingdom He
promised to those who love Him? But you dishonor the
poor! Isn't it the rich who oppress you and drag you into
court? Aren't they the ones who slander Jesus Christ,
whose noble name you bear?*

 JAMES 2:5-7 NLT

Once again, James shows us that we are doing life kind of backward. One illustration might be when we look at a kaleidoscope from the wrong end. We see what looks like broken pieces of something. We can't quite figure out what we are looking at or how to make sense out of it. Perhaps if we were just to do the reverse of popular ideologies and turn our focus around—like we might do with the kaleidoscope—then we would receive clarity and satisfaction and even delight.

Most of the households in America would fall into the top five percent of household incomes in the world.

This verse is a call to examine our hearts and attitudes towards those who are less fortunate. Do we honor and respect them? Let us remember that true wealth lies in our relationship with God and our love for others, regardless of their social or economic standing.

So, while it's easy to fall into the trap of thinking that money will bring us joy, when we look through the right side of the kaleidoscope, colors suddenly go radiant, and chaotic pieces form into exquisite designs. Clarity is ours, and all of it makes sense now. Our ultimate inheritance is not found in earthly riches but in the eternal riches of God's presence and love.

May we turn our perspective around by gazing through God's radiant and living Word. What a world of difference it will make!

Almighty God, I admit I too often let the people
around me influence the way I perceive things,
and it's not always good. I know You've told us that our
ways are not Your ways. Please show me how to see life,
and may it change me and all those around me.
In Jesus's powerful name I pray. Amen.

HELP IN TIMES OF TROUBLE

The Lord is a strong fortress.
The godly run to Him and are safe.

PROVERBS 18:10 TLB

When life feels as if your very soul is being assaulted and there seems to be no escape, no refuge from the onslaught, then run to God. He is your security and a mighty fortress. Psalms reminds us so beautifully, *"God is our refuge and strength [mighty and impenetrable], a very present and well-proved help in trouble"* (46:1 AMP).

Why so many attacks? The answer gets clearer by the year. We are on a long—and sometimes scary—journey, roaming the earth, looking for our final home and for perfect fellowship with God. Our hearts and souls yearn for the way life was meant to be and the way we are promised it will be one day.

Isn't it wonderful that in the meantime—while we wait for Christ's return—God is our help in times of danger and suffering? In the midst of uncertainty and distress, may we each fully embrace the Lord's unfathomable love and reliable strength. We will need every bit of it as we finish our journey toward home.

Almighty God, I call on You to come to my rescue
in these times of earthly trials. I need You every day,
every hour. Thank You that You provide such a mighty
fortress. I cling to You as my God and my King.
I will love You always. In Jesus's powerful name I pray.
Amen.

LOVING
THE UNLOVABLE

*If you really fulfill the royal law according
to the Scripture, "You shall love your neighbor
as yourself," you do well.*

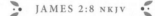 JAMES 2:8 NKJV

James is absolutely set on making us all squirm spiritually, right? Sure, maybe we could find it in ourselves to love our neighbor. In fact, that neighbor might turn out to be a peach of a gal, and you might become close friends. Okay, well, then that's doable. But what does "neighbor" really mean? Even religious scholars in Jesus's time wanted to know the actual definition of *neighbor*—perhaps hoping for a loophole in the midst of such seemingly difficult expectations.

Here's Luke's account: *"Just then a religion scholar stood up with a question to test Jesus. "Teacher, what do I need to do to get eternal life?" He answered, "What's written in God's Law? How do you interpret it?" He said, "That you love the Lord your God with all your passion and prayer and muscle* and intelligence—and that you love your neighbor as well as you do yourself." "Good answer!" said Jesus. "Do it and you'll live." Looking for a loophole, he asked, "And just how would you define 'neighbor'?" (10:25–29 THE MESSAGE).

Jesus went on to tell the famous parable of the Good Samaritan, revealing that everyone is our neighbor, even people we don't particularly like. To read the full story, go to Luke 10:30–37. This story can revolutionize your life spiritually.

So, bottom line—you mean I am supposed to love everyone, even when I don't agree with them? Yes. But God loved each of us even when we were unlovable. And just because we love someone in Christ, that doesn't mean we have to agree with them. There is, indeed, freedom in that truth.

And wouldn't truth and freedom be the best road map to peace and joy?

Lord, to be truly honest,
people can be so hard to love sometimes.
Show me how to care about everyone like You do.
Amen.

A TIME FOR EVERYTHING

Like one who takes away a garment on a cold day,
or like vinegar poured on a wound,
is one who sings songs to a heavy heart.

PROVERBS 25:20 NIV

Have you ever witnessed someone getting emotionally trampled while in the midst of genuine sorrow? For instance, when a friend's husband dies, and somebody shows up at the funeral with a chirpy, "Well, he lived a good, long life." That statement might seem true, but it comes off callous to the one who is grieving. It is truly like pouring vinegar on her wound. Ecclesiastes says it perfectly, *"A time to weep and a time to laugh, a time to mourn and a time to dance"* (3:4 NIV).

Jesus Himself was called a man of sorrows, and He, too, wept while He was here. In the book of Isaiah, we read, *"He was despised and rejected by men, a man of sorrows and acquainted with grief; and as one from whom men hide their faces he was despised, and we* esteemed him not" (53:3 ESV).

May we always be sensitive enough in our spirits to know what time it is—whether it is a time to weep and mourn or a time to laugh and dance. And may all that we do bless others and delight the Lord.

Dear Jesus, teach me how to be more sensitive to the people around me—to my family, friends, colleagues, and well, everyone who crosses my path.
May I not blurt out words that can harm but shower thoughtful words that can heal. And teach me when to speak and when to be quiet and listen. Amen.

ALL THE
GOOD STUFF

*But if you show partiality [prejudice, favoritism],
you are committing sin and are convicted by the
Law as offenders. For whoever keeps the whole Law
but stumbles in one point, he has become guilty of
[breaking] all of it. For He who said, "Do not commit
adultery," also said, "Do not murder." Now if you do
not commit adultery, but you murder, you have become
guilty of transgressing the [entire] Law.*

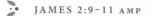

JAMES 2:9-11 AMP

Don't people tend to think of themselves as pretty good people—all in all? We tend to believe our moments of sweetness will cancel out the deeds we might cringe over. You know, the ones that if God put them up on a big silver screen for everyone to see at the theater, we might die of mortification? Yeah, those. But we still notoriously want to believe that people have plenty of good in them that sort of balances things out in the grand scheme of things. We might even get visions of giant celestial scales dancing in our heads as we see each person's noble deeds weighing more heavily on one side than all their not-so-beautiful actions and thoughts on the other.

But then, what on earth do we do with all the Scriptures that say the opposite? Romans reminds us, *"As it is written, None is righteous, just and truthful and upright and conscientious, no, not one"* (3:10 AMPC).

The Word of God is clear: if we break one of God's commandments, we break them all. But thankfully, that is not the end of the story. The joyful news is that through Christ's sacrifice, death, and resurrection, we are offered salvation in Him. We can choose life—full of purpose and fruitfulness and abundance.

Here is a magnificent reminder of this promise in the book of John. *"The thief comes only to steal and kill and destroy. I came that they may have life and have it abundantly"* (10:10 ESV).

Choose Jesus, and you choose abundant life, both now and forevermore!

Dear God, thank You for the abundant life and joy You've given me through Your Son! Amen.

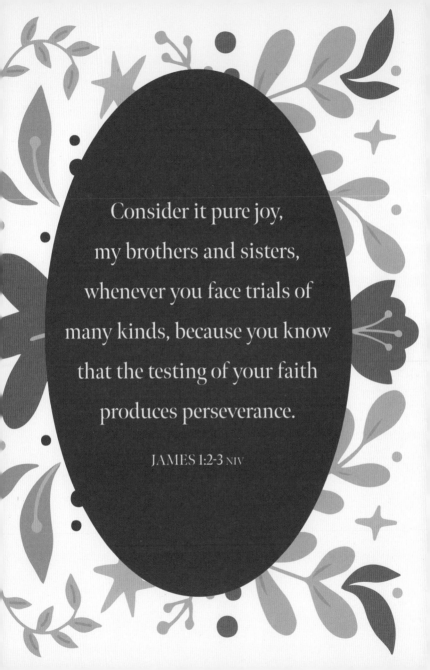

Consider it pure joy,
my brothers and sisters,
whenever you face trials of
many kinds, because you know
that the testing of your faith
produces perseverance.

JAMES 1:2-3 NIV

THE AUTHOR OF LIFE

Listen to your father who gave you life,
and do not despise your mother when she is old.

 PROVERBS 23:22 ESV

So much can be said about life! In fact, good questions on this timeless topic might be, "Is life sacred to us since God is the Author of life?" And too, "Do we honor people, including those who are ill or elderly?" Genesis has such profound and poignant words about life and how we came to be: *"So God created man in his own image, in the image of God he created him; male and female he created them"* (1:27 ESV).

And then Psalms exquisitely announces the preciousness of what God has made: *"For you formed my inward parts; you knitted me together in my mother's womb. I praise you, for I am fearfully and wonderfully made. Wonderful are your works; my soul knows it very well. My frame was not hidden from you, when I was being made in secret, intricately woven in the depths of the earth. Your eyes saw my unformed* substance; in *your book were written, every one of them, the days that were formed for me, when as yet there was none of them*" (139:13–16 ESV).

May we always honor life, since life is a sublime and sacred gift from God!

Lord, may I always honor life and respect people. And thank You for making me in Your image.
What inexpressible joy! Amen.

A VISION
OF MERCY

*Speak and act as those who are going to be judged
by the law that gives freedom, because judgment
without mercy will be shown to anyone who has not
been merciful. Mercy triumphs over judgment.*

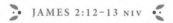

JAMES 2:12-13 NIV

When we think of mercy, oh, how it has the potential to make our shoulders relax and our spirits sigh with relief and joy. How many times has God shown us mercy—when we didn't expect it? And yet there it was. Or when a friend, spouse, or coworker offered us mercy. Maybe we dropped the ball in a big way, leaving a friend in the lurch. Maybe the first time was an accident, but the second time was, well, not an accident. Perhaps we just got a bit lackadaisical or selfish or worse. Then, when we expected a heavy-handed reaction to our shortcomings—or sharp words to really put us in our place—well, mercy arrived, and we thought we might cry a river of gratitude.

These ponderings of thoughtfulness and compassion and tenderness might conjure up a vision of a clear pond on a warm spring day. No rushing waves or harsh sun, just a still, cool surface inviting us to float along, enjoying the dappled sunlight through the trees and the gentlest of breezes. Unwinding never felt so good, knowing that what has gone wrong is being made right through the gift of mercy. We are free to live again, breathe again.

And we have the choice to offer mercy to others. A verse from the book of Luke gently reminds us, *"Be merciful (responsive, compassionate, tender) just as your [heavenly] Father is merciful"* (6:36 AMP).

Whether mercy is given or received—it brings a heart of praise and gladness.

Almighty God, You have shown me great mercy
throughout my whole life. Too many times to count.
I love that about You. Please help me to show that kind
of compassion to others who need it today.
I am willing to be Your ambassador of mercy and joy!
In Jesus's powerful name I pray. Amen.

SACRED MOMENTS

Dear friends, do you think you'll get anywhere in this if you learn all the right words but never do anything? Does merely talking about faith indicate that a person really has it? For instance, you come upon an old friend dressed in rags and half-starved and say, "Good morning, friend! Be clothed in Christ! Be filled with the Holy Spirit!" and walk off without providing so much as a coat or a cup of soup—where does that get you? Isn't it obvious that God-talk without God-acts is outrageous nonsense?

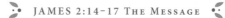 JAMES 2:14–17 THE MESSAGE

After reading these verses, what do we imagine first? Perhaps a homeless man who is sitting on the front steps of our church? Would we wish that person well and then hope he drifts away? Maybe we will say something uplifting or offer a prayer. Then, as he leaves—still hungry—we might send him off with a smile and a wave.

But James might tell us that we've missed a divine opportunity to show this precious man how valuable he is. It is one of those sacred moments when we can show the goodness and light of our Lord. And it's when the rubber meets the road as folks witness a sincere maturity in our faith rather than a bunch of talk. When people know we are Christ-followers and when they see us in a positive action mode, it will wow them into wanting to know more about our Lord.

And in case there is any confusion, James does not mean that we are saved by works. We are saved by grace through faith in Christ. Period. But our faith needs to reflect Christ, and that translates into action. Our gratitude to God for all He's done for us will show in our deeds, including being useable for the Kingdom of God.

How exciting that when we are offered that next divine opportunity, we can shine like the Son!

Jesus, help me to live a life that reflects who You are in all I say and do! Amen.

TO BUILD A GODLY FAMILY!

The wisest of women builds her house,
but folly with her own hands tears it down.

 PROVERBS 14:1 ESV

Having babies is not always easy, and raising them can be a wild adventure as well as an awesome endeavor. As these precious little ones grow up, we must be constantly gathering in and offering godly wisdom. From the very beginning, wise parents lay down a good foundation that is founded on God's Word. And then, of course, we'd want to write His ideals on our hearts and use them as we have need.

First Corinthians tells us, *"For no other foundation can anyone lay than that which is [already] laid, which is Jesus Christ (the Messiah, the Anointed One)"* (3:11 AMPC).

And then there is this encouraging promise in Proverbs: *"Train up a child in the way he should go; even when he is old he will not depart from it"* (22:6 ESV).

When we make Christ the head of our marriage and family, we will please God. And in delighting Him, we will bring delight to our family. Such encouragement. Such joy!

Dear Lord, may I be a woman full of Your wisdom,
and may I always honor all Your holy precepts so that
my children will come to know You and love You
better every day. Thank You that we can build
a family together and that we can all flourish!
In Jesus's powerful name I pray. Amen.

"ALL IN" WITH GOD

But someone will say, "You have faith and I have works."
Show me your faith apart from your works,
and I will show you my faith by my works.

 JAMES 2:18 ESV

A re we "all in" with God?

Once again, James isn't saying we can earn our salvation through works, but he is encouraging Christians to express their faith well, which would include good deeds. In other words, if we love God, let's show it! How can we reflect all the passion we have for our Lord in our daily lives? Jesus approached His disciples with a similar kind of question on the night He was betrayed:

Then He returned to His disciples and found them sleeping. "Couldn't you men keep watch with Me for one hour?" He asked Peter. "Watch and pray so that you will not fall into temptation. The spirit is willing, but the flesh is weak." He went away a second time and prayed, "My Father, if it is not possible for this cup to be taken away unless I drink it, may Your will be done." When He came back, He again found them sleeping, because their eyes were heavy. So He left them and went away once more and prayed the third time, saying the same thing. Then He returned to the disciples and said to them, "Are you still sleeping and resting? Look, the hour has come, and the Son of Man is delivered into the hands of sinners." (Matthew 26:40–45 NIV)

Jesus needed His disciples to be awake during the dark hours before His arrest, but they kept falling asleep! Fortunately, later, they discovered how to be passionately "all in" with Christ. And so, the Gospel message spread in a powerful way.

Wouldn't our life be more of what God desires if we gave Him everything we've got, including godly deeds? If we are "all in" with our Lord, that kind of love can reverberate in our family, in our community, and around the globe.

Dear Lord, show me how to be more in love with You, and may that love flow out as wonderful deeds that glorify You. Amen.

THE SOUL IS SWEETENED

*The heart is delighted by the fragrance of oil
and sweet perfumes, and in just the same way,
the soul is sweetened by the wise counsel of a friend.*

PROVERBS 27:9 THE VOICE

Fragrances can be beguiling and comforting and oh, so memorable. So much so that if your beloved grandmother was known for a particular fragrance and you came across it at a department store counter decades later, you might just burst into tears of joy. Why? Because in an instant, that pleasing aroma has rejoined you with the sweet memories of your dear Gigi.

And so it goes with the wonderment of lovely perfumes. Even if a particular perfume is not connected with anything in our past, the simple joy of a pleasant fragrance can bring us bliss. The book of Proverbs says that just as our heart is delighted by oils and perfumes, so the soul is sweetened by the wise counsel of a friend.

Is that the kind of friends we choose? Ones that

are so wise that their advice sweetens the soul and joy follows close behind them? Looks like choosing the right friends can, indeed, make a huge difference in our lives, because another proverb says, *"Become wise by walking with the wise; hang out with fools and watch your life fall to pieces"* (Proverbs 13:20 The Message).

May we choose friends wisely and may our souls always be sweetened because of it.

Lord, please show me how to
choose my friends wisely. Amen.

MY LIFE STORY

But are you willing to recognize, you foolish [spiritually shallow] person, that faith without [good] works is useless? Was our father Abraham not [shown to be] justified by works [of obedience which expressed his faith] when he offered Isaac his son on the altar [as a sacrifice to God]? You see that [his] faith was working together with his works, and as a result of the works, his faith was completed [reaching its maturity when he expressed his faith through obedience]. And the Scripture was fulfilled which says, "ABRAHAM BELIEVED GOD, AND THIS [faith] WAS CREDITED TO HIM [by God] AS RIGHTEOUSNESS and AS CONFORMITY TO HIS WILL," and he was called the friend of God. You see that a man (believer) is justified by works and not by faith alone [that is, by acts of obedience a born-again believer reveals his faith]. In the same way, was Rahab the prostitute not justified by works too, when she received the [Hebrew] spies as guests and protected them, and sent them away [to escape] by a different route?

JAMES 2:20–25 AMP

People love big, sweeping stories that are true and profound. And obviously James does, too, since he used the Bible stories of Abraham and Rahab to further teach on the importance of good deeds in our daily life. We could see Abraham's faith as it played out in his actions. To read the account in its entirety, go to Genesis 22:1–19.

And the story of Rahab and the way her faith translated into deeds by giving lodging to the spies, well, it's the courageous stuff that makes ordinary people into biblical heroes. And God honored Rahab's deeds in a number of important ways. To be wowed by Rahab's courageous actions, read the whole story in Joshua 2–6.

Once again, James is not saying we are saved by works. But James does remind us that in acts of obedience a born-again believer reveals her faith. In our modern world, are we doers of the Word? Have we shown mercy? Are we brave and loving enough to speak God's truth even when it is not the popular view of the day? With Christ at the helm, our life stories can also become anything but ordinary!

Lord, help my life story to be all You want it to be.
Amen.

TEACHING 101

Not many [of you] should become teachers
[serving in an official teaching capacity], my brothers
and sisters, for you know that we [who are teachers]
will be judged by a higher standard [because we have
assumed greater accountability and more condemnation
if we teach incorrectly].

JAMES 3:1 AMP

Have you ever attended a Bible class with a teacher who bored you so profoundly that you had to sit in the back just in case you fell asleep and snored? Actually, what is far worse than a teacher being mind-numbing, is when you realize he doesn't know what he is talking about. Perhaps his teachings aren't biblically sound, and his words are instead reflecting what he thinks people might like to hear. Maybe he's even promoting the trendy beliefs of the day rather than what God has to say on the subject.

James presents the right way to handle this problem. He says accepting a biblical teaching position nonchalantly is not the road to take. When we instruct, we will be judged by a higher standard than those who are being taught, because we have assumed greater accountability and more condemnation if we lead people astray with false teachings.

Does that mean we need to make a run for it if God has called us to teach? No, not at all. In fact, do you remember the plight of Jonah when he fled from God's mission? Things didn't go well for him until he decided to follow through with the Lord's plan. But this verse in James does need to give us pause before we agree to a biblical teaching position. If we are not prepared, there are plenty of other ways to serve the Lord until we are ready—that is, if and when God calls us to it.

What has God asked you to do? How can you bring Him joy with the talents He has gifted you with? The possibilities can be exciting and filled with purposeful adventure!

Lord, I think You might be calling me to teach.
If this is Your divine will for me, give me a clear sign.
And if You do say yes, please help me to do this
humbling task with grace and knowledge and wisdom.
Amen.

THERE IS REAL HOPE

Don't envy evil men but continue to reverence the Lord all the time, for surely you have a wonderful future ahead of you. There is hope for you yet!

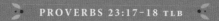 **PROVERBS 23:17–18 TLB**

In times of trouble, we need to cling to hope. Not just a generic hope for better times ahead, for that dream rings empty, and in the end, gains us nothing. But our hope is in the Lord! Second Corinthians give us a beautiful assurance in this: *"He delivered us from such a deadly peril, and he will deliver us. On him we have set our hope that he will deliver us again"* (1:10 ESV).

Jesus helps us with everything if we believe in Him and make our requests known to Him. May we show reverence to Christ and cling steadily to Him, for He is our only hope in redemption and in earthly travails.

Revelation also leaves us with this resplendent promise: *"He will wipe away every tear from their eyes,* and death shall be no more, neither shall there be mourning, nor crying, nor pain anymore, for the former things have passed away" (21:4 ESV).

And all God's people shouted—Amen!

Almighty God, I come before You with all my fears and doubts and sleepless nights, and I place them before You, trusting that You will take my burden and give me peace and hope. I ask all this in the powerful name of my Lord and Savior, Jesus Christ! Amen.

THE DOOR
OF MY LIPS

For we all stumble and sin in many ways.
If anyone does not stumble in what he says
[never saying the wrong thing], he is a perfect man
[fully developed in character, without serious flaws],
able to bridle his whole body and rein in his entire
nature [taming his human faults and weaknesses].

JAMES 3:2 AMP

James really gets straight to it, doesn't he? When he says that we all stumble and sin in many ways, he is painfully right, because unfortunately, stumbling and sinning is common among earthly sojourners.

And one of the whopper errors to which we succumb is when we speak the wrong words. There are so many cringeworthy examples, it is hard to know where to start! How many times have we wounded someone with our words? Too many to count, and sometimes we may not even know we've injured that person until years later. Or perhaps we released bits of gossip because we couldn't control our impulse to tell some juicy tale.

Or, say, we chitchatted on and on with dubious information because we wanted to come off like we were women in the know, but it only monopolized the conversation when the other person might have needed a friend who was really willing to listen. Or perhaps we had a vengeful moment—which we labeled "righteous indignation"—and we spewed the very words that could ruin someone's reputation. Yikes! We have all been guilty of some, if not all of these.

Ephesians reminds us, *"Let no corrupting talk come out of your mouths, but only such as is good for building up, as fits the occasion, that it may give grace to those who hear"* (4:29 ESV).

And then Psalms says, *"Set a guard over my mouth, LORD; keep watch over the door of my lips"* (141:3 NIV).

When we are in need of taming the tongue, we can always ask God for help. He will be the best guard at the door of our lips. May we always desire His attendance!

God, please rein in my tongue, develop my character, and bring me into spiritual maturity. Amen.

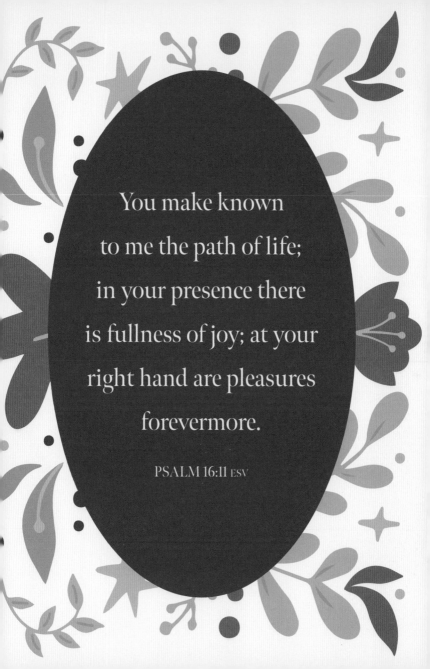

You make known
to me the path of life;
in your presence there
is fullness of joy; at your
right hand are pleasures
forevermore.

PSALM 16:11 ESV

A FINE-TUNED CONSCIENCE

A man's conscience is the Lord's searchlight exposing his hidden motives.

 PROVERBS 20:27 TLB

Our conscience may seem annoying and even maddening at times—that is, when we'd like to do something we shouldn't—but that God-given sense of right and wrong is our friend. We need it!

The last thing we should want to do is to damage or stifle our conscience in any way, since it is the Lord's searchlight, exposing our hidden motives. First Timothy says, *"These teachers will tell lies with straight faces and do it so often that their consciences won't even bother them"* (4:2 TLB).

Just as we like to keep our physical body in good working order, how much more important it is that we keep our conscience in tip-top shape!

Lord Jesus, I admit I am far from perfect,
but I desire to mature in my walk with You.
Help me to keep my conscience fine-tuned and ever
connected with You. Show me how to become the
woman You want me to be, and give me the daily
wisdom and courage to pull it off! Amen.

WE CAN CHOOSE JOY!

When we put bits into the mouths of horses to make them obey us, we can turn the whole animal. Or take ships as an example. Although they are so large and are driven by strong winds, they are steered by a very small rudder wherever the pilot wants to go.

JAMES 3:3-4 NIV

Yes, horses can be made to obey with a bit, and a ship can be turned with a small rudder, but the tongue seems harder to control—as James reminds us—than just about anything!

But the good news is that we do have a choice. A minute-by-minute choice, really, on what spews from our mouths. And when we choose wisely, it can be so fine. We can get a glimpse of heaven. Say, a friend walks up to you to meet you for lunch, and for some reason she is sporting a ghastly hairstyle. Visions of cartoon characters are coming to mind. The brutal part of you wants to say, "What were you thinking?" But you know you have to find that delicate balance of politeness and honesty. So, since you like her dress, you instead say, "I love your dress. It's a great color on you!"

Your friend smiles. You made her day. You smile. You both feel great. Life is good. As we all know, with careless words, it could have gone so much differently. The book of Matthew gives us an apt reminder when it says, *"I tell you, on the day of judgment people will give account for every careless word they speak"* (12:36 ESV).

Yes, we are the captains, and if we put God at the helm, then we can navigate into waters full of healing and blessing, comfort and encouragement. We can be changed. People around us can be changed, even the course of history—with mere words. What a splendid thing to ponder.

Why not today—this very day—make the angels rejoice, and God smile, by choosing the right words and choosing joy?

Lord, I confess to You right now that I don't always choose the right words. I too often let my emotions run wild and say whatever comes to mind. I no longer want to live that way. Show me a new way to live, to speak, and to please You in all I do. Amen.

THE WORLD UP IN SMOKE

It only takes a spark, remember, to set off a forest fire.
A careless or wrongly placed word out of your mouth
can do that. By our speech we can ruin the world, turn
harmony to chaos, throw mud on a reputation, send the
whole world up in smoke and go up in smoke with it.

JAMES 3:5-6 THE MESSAGE

O ur tongues can be like flamethrowers, sending out blazing plumes of fire that can consume in minutes. Or our words can be… One. Tiny. Spark. But just as it only takes one match or spark to destroy a whole forest, a flicker of fire can also ignite and destroy a marriage, a lifelong friendship, an entire business, a church, a career, a revival, a ministry, or whatever else gets in the way of our injurious blather.

Imagine such far-reaching ruin that can come from a handful of words. And it all could have been prevented so easily. The book of Colossians also says it well: *"Let your conversation be gracious as well as sensible, for then you will have the right answer for everyone"*

(4:6 TLB). There is a word mentioned in that verse that doesn't come up much anymore—gracious. What a heavenly word. May we ponder its meaning, and may it so permeate our souls that we begin to speak and live and love the way God intended...

Dear God, I have done it again!
I have been spouting off, and I have made a mess of things. Why do I keep doing this? Please forgive me and give me the courage to go to my friend and ask for forgiveness. This can be so humbling and painful, but I know it is also freeing and healing. With Your supernatural help, I want to find a new way to live, to learn from my mistakes, and to move forward in graciousness and wisdom. In Jesus's powerful and holy name I pray. Amen.

FLOWING LIKE SPRING WATER

Knowledge flows like spring water from the wise;
fools are leaky faucets, dripping nonsense.

 PROVERBS 15:2 THE MESSAGE

Have you ever had to sit and listen to a dripping faucet? The incessant, echoing monotony of it will make you want to do something wild-eyed and desperate. And oh, how similar that situation is if you've ever been forced to listen to someone who is spouting foolish nonsense. Maybe it's your boss, or your friend, or maybe it's you! Run for your life, except you can't do that if the guilty party is you!

Seriously, some people seem to have a real aptitude for claptrap, and then others take their pontification on a darker journey by choosing to become false teachers and prophets. Better to run for your life than to listen to their words. In I John, we learn, *"Dear friends, do not believe every spirit, but test the spirits to see whether they are from God, because many false prophets have gone out into the world"* (4:1 NIV).

We need to be on our guard, making sure no one is leading us astray with any kind of teachings that are contrary to the Word of God. May we instead be among the wise, and may knowledge flow from us like spring water.

Lord Jesus, sometimes I think I am just fumbling around in life without knowing what to do next. I'm in great need of knowledge and wisdom so I will know the way I should go. I look forward to Your divine help. Amen.

THERE GOES THAT TONGUE AGAIN!

This is scary: You can tame a tiger, but you can't tame a tongue—it's never been done. The tongue runs wild, a wanton killer. With our tongues we bless God our Father; with the same tongues we curse the very men and women He made in His image. Curses and blessings out of the same mouth! My friends, this can't go on. A spring doesn't gush fresh water one day and brackish the next, does it? Apple trees don't bear strawberries, do they? Raspberry bushes don't bear apples, do they? You're not going to dip into a polluted mud hole and get a cup of clear, cool water, are you?

JAMES 3:7–12 THE MESSAGE

James really must want us to understand this taming-of-the-tongue concept since he dwells on it to make certain we "get it." Bottom line—wouldn't life be far more God-pleasing and beautiful and simply easier to deal with if we followed James's teachings?

A scene comes to mind sparked from James's teaching—and that scene starts out so innocently. Say, you are breezing your way out of church one bright morning, and as you stroll to the car, you stop to hug a friend. Just to have something to say that might be laced with intrigue, you venture the words, "You know, it's really too bad about the music at our church. You'll never believe what I heard…" Immediately your friend perks up and leans closer to you to hear what tidbit you might say. And so there goes that untamed tongue again!

Yes, out of the same mouth can come goodness and mercy and also muckiness and malice.

It's helpful to know that praying for guidance concerning this issue is not a onetime prayer, but a daily seeking of the Lord's help. And the reassuring part is knowing that God really wants us to be victorious in this divine endeavor, so that we can be happy and live a joy-filled life.

Dear Lord, I am bone-tired of cleaning up my endless verbal messes. This kind of living can't go on anymore. I need divine guidance in knowing when to speak, what to say, and when to be quiet. Amen.

WALKING HUMBLY WITH MY GOD

If you are wise and understand God's ways,
prove it by living an honorable life, doing good works
with the humility that comes from wisdom.

JAMES 3:13 NLT

Sometimes we get so caught up in our surroundings that we start to believe that we're better than others. And doesn't it seem as if when we start thinking we are better than others, or deserve more than others, or we should be treated differently than others, God has a way of reminding us that we are equal in His sight? Just as Jesus walked among the lowly and marginalized, showing compassion and love to all, we are called to emulate His example.

The book of Luke reminds us, *"He [Jesus] went on to tell a story to the guests around the table. Noticing how each had tried to elbow into the place of honor, He said, 'When someone invites you to dinner, don't take the place of honor. Somebody more important than you might have been invited by the host. Then he'll* come and call out in front of everybody, "You're in the wrong place. The place of honor belongs to this man." Embarrassed, you'll have to make your way to the very last table, the only place left. When you're invited to dinner, go and sit at the last place. Then when the host comes he may very well say, "Friend, come up to the front." That will give the dinner guests something to talk about! What I'm saying is, If you walk around all high and mighty, you're going to end up flat on your face. But if you're content to be simply yourself, you will become more than yourself'" (14:7–11 THE MESSAGE).

So, maybe high and mighty is not the way to go, then. It won't win a lot of friends, and it won't help fulfill all the incredible things God has for us. It is super easy to dip into the popular mindset that says, *Well, if I don't promote myself, who will?* But God has a better way to live if we will humble ourselves and walk with Him.

Dear God, I am not always a humble woman,
but I desire to be. I want to be all that You created me
to be, and in that, I know there is joy!
In Jesus's name I pray. Amen.

HOLD ME FAST, LORD!

The fear of man brings a snare,
but whoever trusts in and puts his confidence
in the LORD will be exalted and safe.

PROVERBS 29:25 AMP

Have you ever felt as if a dark cloud is sort of following you around? Or maybe you get the niggling sensation that the other shoe is about to drop—and you think that shoe might be anything but nice or wearable?

We have all been there, especially in the darkest hours of the night. Where do we turn for deliverance? The book of Psalms beautifully reminds us where we can go in times of evil and trouble: *"Who stood up for me against the wicked? Who took my side against evil workers? If GOD hadn't been there for me, I never would have made it. The minute I said, 'I'm slipping, I'm falling,' Your love, GOD, took hold and held me fast. When I was upset and beside myself, You calmed me down and cheered me up"* (94:16–19 THE MESSAGE).

And another psalm tells us, *"Because he holds fast to me in love, I will deliver him; I will protect him, because he knows my name. When he calls to me, I will answer him; I will be with him in trouble; I will rescue him and honor him"* (91:14–15 ESV).

These are powerful promises. God is always on the throne, and the Lord God Almighty gets the last say. Try making the Psalms into prayers. God is far more than a good listener; He is also our Deliverer and Rescuer.

Lord, these days I need a daily rescue in one way or the other. Please hold me fast! Amen.

SACRED PROMISES

But if you are bitterly jealous and there is
selfish ambition in your heart,
don't cover up the truth with boasting and lying.

JAMES 3:14 NLT

This brief verse covers a lot of serious ground, and the dirt described is full of land mines. This passage in James describes sinning and then adding more sin on top to cover the original sin. Oh my. We might clutch our pearls and ask, "I mean, who could actually live like that?" Well, actually, we all have—from time to time.

We will have to own up to these patterns if we want to welcome real change. Even common sense would say, "Who really wants to live a life riddled with jealousy, selfishness, boasting, and lying?" Sounds like a good way to become not only spiritually sick, but emotionally and physically ill too.

For instance, when we make the choice to compare ourselves with others, it will only breed trouble, and that green-eyed goblin that rises up in us can easily escalate into something even more monstrous. Maybe to stop all this downward spiral of the soul, we could make this Scripture in Jeremiah a memory verse: *"For I know the plans I have for you, says the Lord. They are plans for good and not for evil, to give you a future and a hope"* (29:11 TLB).

Wouldn't it be splendid to take God at His Word? To place His sacred promises deep in your heart, where they can make a daily difference? What one-of-a-kind design do you think the Lord has planned for you? If you don't know, now is always a good time to ask...

Dear Lord, please give me Your supernatural strength to walk away from these tendencies and fly free with You. I know that what You have planned for me is good, and it will bring me a future and a hope. Please show me the way. Amen.

WON'T IT ALL
LOOK HEAVENLY?

This is not the wisdom that comes down from above,
but is earthly, unspiritual, demonic.

JAMES 3:15 ESV

Well, after reading this verse and the previous verse from James, we might bristle a bit. I mean, surely none of us would do anything that could actually be labeled with such a dark term—like *demonic*. And yet, James would say these choices—such as jealousy, selfish ambition, boasting, and lying, which are mentioned earlier—are devilish in nature rather than helpful and healing and holy. God does not want us to go on living in a way that will lead to destruction, but He wants us to live His way, which will instead bring refreshment, encouragement, maturity, and delight. And isn't it just like our loving Lord to help us exit such a ruinous path and put us on a journey to life, love, and joy?

Colossians says it so stunningly well: *"So, chosen by God for this new life of love, dress in the wardrobe God picked out for you: compassion, kindness, humility,* quiet strength, discipline. Be even-tempered, content with second place, quick to forgive an offense. Forgive as quickly and completely as the Master forgave you. And regardless of what else you put on, wear love. It's your basic, all-purpose garment. Never be without it" (3:12–14 THE MESSAGE).

All those virtues will be like beautiful spiritual apparel as they drape across our lives! And what about forgiveness? May we forgive quickly and completely as the Master has forgiven us. And may love always be our most basic gown of choice. Won't it all look heavenly?

Dear God, I still have a long way to go in my spiritual journey. Show me all the many ways I can choose rightly, and may I always go out of the house wearing love! In Jesus's hallowed name I pray. Amen.

WHAT A WAY
TO LIVE!

*For where jealousy and selfish ambition exist,
here will be disorder and every vile practice.*

> JAMES 3:16 ESV

Selfish ambition could be considered a common sin whether we're talking about ancient times or modern days. Either way, God is trying to push us to be our best and rid us of anything that is not like His character. And why not? We are the salt and light of the world.

Here is a scene to highlight the concept. What if your coworker put herself out there as a strong Christ follower, and yet you saw her slyly trying to demolish someone else's chances for a raise and a promotion? You watch her in action, and with all the finagling and boasting, you realize she will do just about anything to achieve her goal. She seems capable of squashing quite a few toes as she shoves and stomps her way up that ladder of success. After all, she believes that God wants her to prosper in every way. Plotting and then labeling it holy is not a wise way to live. Here is a more elaborate reminder from James in *The Message*:

Do you want to be counted wise, to build a reputation for wisdom? Here's what you do: Live well, live wisely, live humbly. It's the way you live, not the way you talk, that counts. Mean-spirited ambition isn't wisdom. Boasting that you are wise isn't wisdom. Twisting the truth to make yourselves sound wise isn't wisdom. It's the furthest thing from wisdom—it's animal cunning, devilish plotting. Whenever you're trying to look better than others or get the better of others, things fall apart and everyone ends up at the others' throats" (3:13–16 THE MESSAGE)

Simple, straightforward living brings order out of chaos, chooses truth instead of lies, and replaces hate with love. So, may we live well and live wisely...

Dear Jesus, unfortunately I have been guilty of selfish ambition and some of the accompanying sins that go with it. Forgive me. Help me instead to encourage others and to lift them up. May my Christian witness be so strong that people will want to know more about You and Your mercy and grace! Amen.

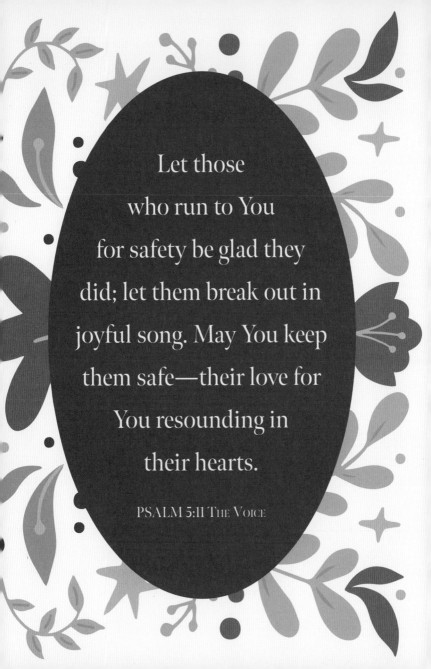

Let those who run to You for safety be glad they did; let them break out in joyful song. May You keep them safe—their love for You resounding in their hearts.

PSALM 5:11 THE VOICE

THE SMARTEST PERSON

To respond to a matter before you hear about it
shows foolishness and brings shame.

 PROVERBS 18:13 THE VOICE

People like to make you think they are brilliant and educated and dazzling. They like to be people of information who are desperately needed. But in reality, they tend to come off like pesky know-it-alls. And that never looks good. Why? Because smarty pants and clever clogs are not easy to live with, work with, or even have lunch with! They want to pontificate while you spend all your time agreeing with them and telling them how wonderful they are. Yet when you look into the barrel of their vast wisdom and experience, the tub echoes because it is mostly empty!

Proverbs tells us that some people even want to answer you before they get all the facts. They jump in full throttle with the answer, and they may not even know the full question. What nonsense. But they can't see it. What a shame.

Actually, Proverbs says this mode of talking brings on shame and disgrace. Humiliation is the opposite impression these folks are trying to make. So, what brings on all this human folly? Pride? Poor self-esteem? A craving for acceptance and love? Hard to know, since each person is so different, but we can certainly pray for them, and also pray that we don't become ensnared in the same type of nonsense.

Sometimes the smartest person in the room is the one being quiet!

Dear Lord, show me when to speak
and when to be quiet. Amen.

USABLE FOR
ALL THINGS
WONDERFUL

But the wisdom that comes from heaven is first of all pure; then peace-loving, considerate, submissive, full of mercy and good fruit, impartial and sincere.

 JAMES 3:17 NIV

Have you ever strolled through a vineyard or an orchard and relished—maybe even swooned— over all the juicy, sweet fruit when it was ripe and ready for harvest? Nothing else is quite like it. You reach up and pluck a pear from the tree and bite right into it. The juice bursts from the fruit, and maybe you let the nectar run down your chin just for the fun of it. Ahh, so delicious. Now it's time to gather in a basket load to take home for preserves or compote or cobbler or anything else you can dream up. Wouldn't it be wonderful if people saw us that way as followers of Christ—as folks who are wholesome and inviting and bursting with goodness?

So, how in the world can we become good and sweet fruit? Jesus gives us some more answers: *"I am the Vine, you are the branches. When you're joined with Me and I with you, the relation intimate and organic, the harvest is sure to be abundant. Separated, you can't produce a thing. Anyone who separates from Me is deadwood, gathered up and thrown on the bonfire. But if you make yourselves at home with Me and My words are at home in you, you can be sure that whatever you ask will be listened to and acted upon. This is how My Father shows who He is—when you produce grapes, when you mature as My disciples"* (John 15:5–8 THE MESSAGE).

Ahhh, so sweet. So beautiful. And usable for all things good, all things wonderful. And why? Because we stayed connected to the Source of all sustenance—God.

Father God, I desire to be the good fruit You speak of in Your holy Word. I want to have wisdom and purity and sincerity. I want to be a peacemaker, considerate, submissive, impartial, and full of mercy and good fruit. But I can only accomplish this if I stay attached securely to You. May it always be so! In Jesus's name I pray.
Amen.

SURPRISE YOUR ENEMIES

If you see your enemy hungry, go buy him lunch;
if he's thirsty, bring him a drink. Your generosity will
surprise him with goodness, and GOD will look after you.

PROVERBS 25:21-22 THE MESSAGE

After reading this verse in Proverbs and seeing the word *surprise*, we might be tempted to think of a sudden verbal assault as in retribution, since that is what people tend to think of in connection with an enemy. But God says to do the opposite—such as *surprise* her with goodness. Perhaps buy her lunch if she is hungry. Really? Isn't that going a bit too far? Not according to God.

Now it is easier to see that the books of James and Proverbs show us that living the Lord's way does not always follow the popular trends of the day. In the book of Matthew, Jesus tells us, *"There is a saying, 'Love your friends and hate your enemies.' But I say: Love your enemies! Pray for those who persecute you! In that way you will be acting as true sons of your Father in heaven. For He gives His sunlight to both the evil and the good, and sends rain on the just and on the unjust too"* (5:43–45 TLB).

Who are your enemies? What goodness can you offer them today? Praying for them is always a good place to start.

Lord, the last thing on earth I want to do is love my enemies, and yet I want to please You always. Show me the way. Amen.

GOODWILL TOWARD MEN

And the seed whose fruit is righteousness
(spiritual maturity) is sown in peace by those who
make peace [by actively encouraging goodwill
between individuals].

JAMES 3:18 AMP

There is a memorable verse in Luke that reads, *"Glory to God in the highest, and on earth peace, goodwill toward men"* (2:14 NKJV). Don't you just love that?

Why do these words melt our hearts every time we hear them in this verse or in the famous Christmas carol? Maybe because deep in our souls we know this is how humans were supposed to live. It is a sacred concept, yes, and it is the way of heaven.

The book of Matthew reminds us, *"You're blessed when you can show people how to cooperate instead of compete or fight. That's when you discover who you really are, and your place in God's family"* (5:9 THE MESSAGE). Yes, blessed are those peacemakers. What a benevolent and beneficial way to show our love for Christ.

The book of Romans tells us, *"If possible, so far as it depends on you, live peaceably with all"* (12:18 ESV).

Pray for peace. Live in peace, if possible. And then that great Scripture and song will always ring in our ears, even when it is not Christmastime—*"on earth peace, goodwill toward men."* May it be our heart's prayer every day of every year. It will change us and have a divine ripple effect that never ends…

Jesus, there are days when I don't feel a lot of goodwill toward anyone, especially people who are causing me grief! And it sometimes seems like goodwill is only a memory from a bygone era. But we are made in Your image, and our souls still crave peace. Please make me a peacemaker. Amen.

HIS NAME IS JESUS

*There are six things that the LORD hates, seven that are
an abomination to him: haughty eyes, a lying tongue,
and hands that shed innocent blood, a heart that
devises wicked plans, feet that make haste to run to
evil, a false witness who breathes out lies,
and one who sows discord among brothers.*

 **PROVERBS 6:16–19 ESV**

When we finish reading this list in Proverbs of seven things the Lord considers to be an abomination, we can admit this is far from light reading. Still, we have all known sin's dark realities, and we know in our souls that to embrace even one of these transgressions is to disinvite joy in our lives.

No matter what we've done, though, our souls will always yearn for happiness with the Lord! How marvelous it is that in the book of I John, God's Word says, *"But if we confess our sins to Him, He can be depended on to forgive us and to cleanse us from every wrong. And it is perfectly proper for God to do this for us because Christ died to wash away our sins"* (1:9 TLB).

What can be more wonderful than a verse like this after the heaviest of verses above that? Yes, there is a divine fix to this epic problem of the soul—and His name is Jesus.

Dear Jesus, I can't thank You enough or praise You enough or love You enough for all You've done for me. With Your very life, You paid the price on the cross to redeem me from all my sins. And because I have accepted Your gift of salvation, I now look forward to heaven with You forever! Amen.

THE REAL DEAL

What is causing the quarrels and fights among you?
Don't they come from the evil desires at war within you?
You want what you don't have, so you scheme and kill to
get it. You are jealous of what others have, but you can't
get it, so you fight and wage war to take it away from
them. Yet you don't have what you want because you
don't ask God for it. And even when you ask, you don't
get it because your motives are all wrong—you want
only what will give you pleasure. You adulterers! Don't
you realize that friendship with the world makes you an
enemy of God? I say it again: If you want to be a friend
of the world, you make yourself an enemy of God.

 JAMES 4:1-4 NLT

If you've ever witnessed a toddler in full screeching, stomping mode, wow, it is a distressing sight to see. If you are a mom dealing with this wild, explosive affair, say, in a store or a restaurant, people may start whispering and giving you the evil eye. Someone may even ask you to take your little red-faced dumpling outside!

Adults are fully capable of pulling these kinds of stunts, too, but most have learned how to be quieter and sneakier and more sophisticated about it. But when God sees it, well, it still looks like that wailing, red-faced routine. You know, "I want what I want. Now!"

Why do we carry on so? Some of the time, we're mad because we can't get what we want when we want it—like the toddler. And when we finally do run to God asking for what we think we must have, well—like the toddler's demand—perhaps what we're screaming for is ultimately going to harm us. It might even be something that God strongly opposes. What does that say about our motives?

Drawing nearer to God is the way to alleviate these worldly spiritual pangs. We can always be assured that whatever God wants for us is always the very best. For what God wants is no counterfeit peace or joy, but the real deal!

Lord, when I ask for things, help me to be wise.
I don't want to be a friend to this world, but a friend
to You. Be ever near me, Jesus. Amen.

EMBRACE THE DISCIPLINE

For the LORD corrects those He loves,
just as a father corrects a child in whom he delights.

 PROVERBS 3:12 NLT

Here's a scene you don't see often. A child is disciplined for eating too many cookies before dinner when he was told not to, and the child suddenly says, "Thanks, Mom. I am glad you let me know when I am doing bad stuff and then send me to my room!"

Hard to even imagine that scene playing out. Kids don't generally like rebukes. And adults don't either. Most people just like to be told they are on the correct path in life and doing all the right things. That they are wonderful and pleasing to all those around them—including God, of course. Yes, we not only hate rebukes, but we crave kudos and compliments, even if we don't deserve them. But how can we grow and improve and become all that God wants us to be if we never hear a correction when it's necessary?

We love our kids deeply, and we discipline them because of that love. We want the absolute best for them. And so it goes with God and His loving ways. He wants the absolute best for us, and so He will not leave us in our miserable ways. He wants us to know joy and know it in its fullest.

Lord, I may not be too happy about Your corrections, but I want to be. Show me how to embrace Your divine discipline, for I want more joy for me and for You! Amen.

THE LOVER OF YOUR SOUL

Or do you suppose that the Scripture is speaking to no purpose that says, The Spirit Whom He has caused to dwell in us yearns over us and He yearns for the Spirit [to be welcome] with a jealous love? But He gives us more and more grace (power of the Holy Spirit, to meet this evil tendency and all others fully). That is why He says, God sets Himself against the proud and haughty, but gives grace [continually] to the lowly (those who are humble enough to receive it).

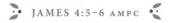

JAMES 4:5-6 AMPC

God loves us with a great passion, far beyond what we can comprehend. And when we fall in love with the Lord and say yes to His redemptive grace, we are His. We are bought with a price—that is, from the sacrifice of Christ on the cross.

And when we choose Jesus, it is a relationship like none other. It is a daily walk, but sometimes on that stroll, we stray off the road. Every day, countless enticements can romance us, pulling us away from Him. But because we are believers, the Holy Spirit—whom the Lord has placed within us—yearns for us to mature and grow and not veer off the course! Venturing one step away from the path can seem so innocent, but many times a single stride leads to another. And another. Until we may no longer even recognize our surroundings or the footpath or even the Lover of our soul who is still wooing us back.

Maybe we have forgotten what joy there was to be had right close by His side. Rejoining Him is only a prayer away...

Dear Jesus, when I allow myself to get too busy or too locked up with all the fearsome things the world throws at me, I lose my spiritual focus, and I get off the amazing course You have set before me. Bring me back to You. I love You, Lord Jesus. Amen.

JOY WILL FLOW THROUGH US

*So submit yourselves to the one true God
and fight against the devil and his schemes.
If you do, he will run away in failure.*

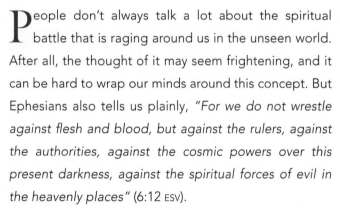

JAMES 4:7 THE VOICE

People don't always talk a lot about the spiritual battle that is raging around us in the unseen world. After all, the thought of it may seem frightening, and it can be hard to wrap our minds around this concept. But Ephesians also tells us plainly, *"For we do not wrestle against flesh and blood, but against the rulers, against the authorities, against the cosmic powers over this present darkness, against the spiritual forces of evil in the heavenly places"* (6:12 ESV).

So, we are not only struggling against a fallen world and our own failings, but we're also dealing with the spiritual forces of evil. This can sound pretty daunting and hopeless. What can be done?

James tells us that when we fight against the devil and his schemes, he will have to flee. Also, First Peter reminds us, *"Be sober [well balanced and self-disciplined], be alert and cautious at all times. That enemy of yours, the devil, prowls around like a roaring lion [fiercely hungry], seeking someone to devour"* (5:8 AMP).

Reading God's Word, staying connected to the Lord in prayer, and remaining close to a body of believers in worship and fellowship are also ways to keep ourselves on course and away from the enemy.

When we are fully engaged with Christ, we will not want to follow the enemy. The more we live in this new way, the more joy will flow through us. And with Christ in us, we are promised a happy ending. Second Timothy promises, *"The Lord will rescue me from every evil deed and bring me safely into his heavenly kingdom. To him be the glory forever and ever. Amen"* (4:18 ESV).

A happy ending, indeed!

Lord, some days I am worn out from all that is going on around me. Keep me on the right course, Jesus.
Keep me safe from the enemy. And, oh, I am so looking forward to being with You in heaven someday! Amen.

A FEAST OF GLOATING

Whoever mocks the poor insults his Maker;
he who is glad at calamity will not go unpunished.

PROVERBS 17:5 ESV

Temptations tend to plague us daily. All varieties. Everyone has different weaknesses when it comes to spiritual failings, but all of them—if we give in to them—will take us away from God, not closer.

Some mock the poor or look at them with disdain, but this attitude insults our Lord, for He cares deeply for them. In fact, the Lord has asked us to help the poor, not ridicule them.

And how tempting it is to gloat. Perhaps someone you know has fallen into trouble because they refused wise guidance—or maybe *your* advice. Or maybe calamity hit when they took the wrong path. We know that we are all subject to God's biblical justice and discipline, but we can acknowledge this truth without finding pleasure or delight in someone else's disaster.

Obadiah reminds us, *"Do not enter the gate of My people in the day of their disaster; yes, you, do not look [with delight] on their misery in the day of their ruin, and do not loot treasures in the day of their ruin"* (1:13 AMP).

May we follow truth and justice but also the kindhearted ideals taught in God's perfect Word.

*Dear Lord, sometimes I feel righteous indignation and
even vindication in this life, but show me when I've
allowed these emotions to slide into sin.
I never want to grieve Your Holy Spirit. Amen.*

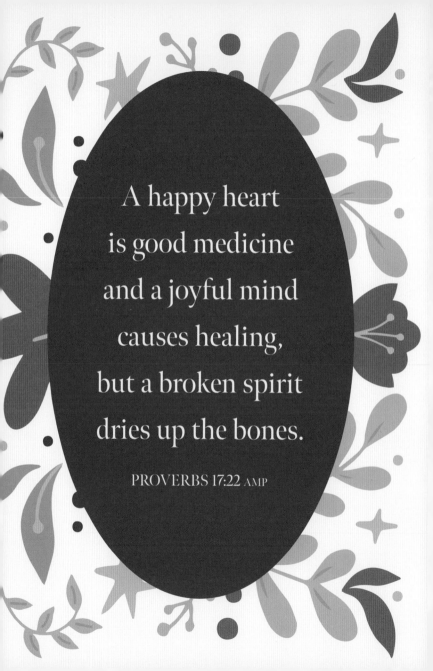

A happy heart
is good medicine
and a joyful mind
causes healing,
but a broken spirit
dries up the bones.

PROVERBS 17:22 AMP

CLAMORING FOR
A MESSAGE

Come close to God, and God will come close to you.
Wash your hands, you sinners; purify your hearts,
for your loyalty is divided between God and the world.

> JAMES 4:8 NLT

If you saw a bottle bobbing in the ocean, and you knew it had a direct message to you from God—what would you do? Most likely you'd hurriedly wade out deeper into the water and snatch it up before it drifted away. You would hold it tight, safely bring it to shore, and then pour over the sacred note that you somehow know will bring you closer to God.

But what if the note said something you didn't like? What if, in the hope of getting closer to God, you had to endure a rebuke and a request for repentance? Hmmm. In that case, you might be tempted to toss the bottle back into the sea, thinking maybe that message was meant for someone else. But if we're sincere about desiring God's intimacy and guidance, then wouldn't we try to follow through with whatever His words said to do, even if it meant we needed to confess our sins before Him? (And as far as clamoring for a message from God, well, we have a whole Book of *real* messages from God—for you and me—called the Bible.)

So, after we choose to repent from whatever is keeping us from being close to our Lord, what do we do next? Spending time fellowshipping with Jesus is the perfect thing to do. And on the topic of fidelity, are we truly loyal to Christ, or do we sometimes want to hang on to unhealthy habits? Contrary to what we've heard, we really can't have it all. We have to choose. Whom will we love and adore? Whom do we follow no matter what other people say? Whom do we want to spend all of eternity with?

Jesus?

Yes, Jesus is the one choice in this life we will never regret.

Dear God, I am always clamoring for a direct message from You, but sometimes I think if I got quiet and really listened for Your voice, I would hear You loud and clear!
I want to draw near to You now, Lord. As You have promised, please draw near to me. I love You. Amen.

THE WAY
TO VICTORY

[As you draw near to God] be deeply penitent and
grieve, even weep [over your disloyalty].
Let your laughter be turned to grief and your mirth to
dejection and heartfelt shame [for your sins].

JAMES 4:9 AMPC

People cry a lot, but sometimes their tears are misplaced. We might be crying because our numbers have stopped climbing on social media. Maybe we are stressed because our likes or hits or views or shares or whatever are plummeting. Or perhaps we just bought an expensive pair of designer shoes that actually clash with that new designer purse. Imagine! Yes, life can be disappointing in a hundred different ways, but true sorrow and weeping need to be reserved for what is important. And according to James, one reason to grieve is when we have been disloyal to Christ.

When we are dillydallying in various sins, we are, indeed, being unfaithful to our beloved Christ. Shouldn't we feel sorrow over sin after all He has done for us on the cross? But you might wonder—well, after grieving and renewal, when is it time to be filled with joy again? The book of Nehemiah speaks on that very topic after the people passed through a time of true repentance:

And Nehemiah, who was the governor, and Ezra the priest and scribe, and the Levites who taught the people said to all the people, "This day is holy to the LORD your God; do not mourn or weep." For all the people wept as they heard the words of the Law. Then he said to them, "Go your way. Eat the fat and drink sweet wine and send portions to anyone who has nothing ready, for this day is holy to our Lord. And do not be grieved, for the joy of the LORD is your strength." So the Levites calmed all the people, saying, "Be quiet, for this day is holy; do not be grieved." (Nehemiah 8:9–11 ESV)

God wants us to live victorious, joy-filled lives, and His holy Word gives us the blueprint to victory!

Dear Lord, after a time of true repentance, show me the way to victory in You! Amen.

A LIE-FREE ZONE

The LORD detests lying lips,
but He delights in people who are trustworthy.

> **PROVERBS 12:22 NIV**

To pull off a string of lies would be almost comical if it weren't so evil. It does take a tremendous amount of brainpower and a mind like a steel trap to keep up with our lies once they get steamrolling. There is the question of whom we told lies to. Then there is the question of how many topics we lied about with each person. And then when we're caught in the lies—which we invariably will be—there is that quick thinking we have to pull off to make the new lies fit the old ones. By then, we are exhausted even thinking about this.

If so, it will make it that much easier to live without them. The book of Colossians tells us, *"Do not lie to one another, for you have stripped off the old self with its evil practices, and have put on the new [spiritual] self who is being continually renewed in true knowledge in the image of Him who created the new self"* (3:9–10 AM P).

So clear. So simple, really. And making our lives a lie-free zone will bring us more joy.

Choose joy!

Lord, I admit that sometimes I have lied.
I try to feel better about the lies by telling myself I had
good reasons for them, but in the end, they were still
lies. Forgive me. I want to be trustworthy in all I say
and do. Help me always to speak the truth in love.
Amen.

HOW TO LIVE

Humble yourselves [feeling very insignificant] in the presence of the Lord, and He will exalt you [He will lift you up and make your lives significant].

> ∴ JAMES 4:10 AMPC ∵

Who wants to think of herself as insignificant? You know, basically someone who's considered of no consequence? Maybe even kind of invisible? Usually, even a shy person who doesn't enjoy the limelight would get her hackles up over such a prospect. I mean, nobody wants to be a nobody!

We like to think we could make life perfect with a stellar self-esteem. There are seminars on the subject, not to mention a zillion how-to books. Self-assurance or self-confidence, well, it is a massive industry, and yet, just as soon as we place the word *self* into the mix, things start to go wonky. For instance, after blowing ourselves up like puffer fish, and swimming in the cool but shallow waters of self-sufficiency, don't we—in all honesty—still feel like helpless minnows in a deep blue sea? Second Corinthians reveals another facet of these divine mysteries: *"But he said to me, 'My grace is sufficient for you, for my power is made perfect in weakness.' Therefore I will boast all the more gladly of my weaknesses, so that the power of Christ may rest upon me"* (12:9 ESV).

Wow, a lot of what James and the rest of the Bible is saying is that we need a new way to perceive ourselves. A brand-new way to live. So, what are we to be, then? Are we insignificant or exalted? Are we weak or powerful?

Well, we are to be humble before the Lord, and then He will lift us up and make our lives significant. And when we are weak, the Lord's power is made perfect in us. How wonderful it is that His grace is sufficient! And don't we have a new lightness of heart and a livelier step knowing we do not have to walk this life alone—but that we can walk with the Lord in His glorious ways? What sacred mysteries and what joy divine!

Lord, thank You that Your living Word shows me
how to think of myself and how to live! Amen.

NAVIGATING THE WORLD WITH GRACE

*Don't bad-mouth each other, friends. It's God's Word,
His Message, His Royal Rule, that takes a beating in
that kind of talk. You're supposed to be honoring the
Message, not writing graffiti all over it. God is in charge
of deciding human destiny. Who do you think you are to
meddle in the destiny of others?*

JAMES 4:11–12 THE MESSAGE

If you have ever been to a once-beautiful city that has
been marred and defaced by graffiti, the sight is truly
alarming and disheartening. More than that, it can get
you riled up with a serious case of righteous indignation
at all the unnecessary destruction of what was once
quite wonderful to behold! Yes, what was grand and
resplendent is now trashed and left for the wind to howl
through it as if it were in some lonely wilderness. The
thing is, it never needs to be that way. There is a choice.

That is a pretty intense but suitable image of how it

can look and feel in a person's life when someone else defaces him or her verbally with slander. Perhaps that criticism stole her smile and her joy. Maybe it went so far as to bring about the loss of her God-given calling, her marriage, or her friends. In the book of Matthew, Jesus says it stunningly well: *"So in everything, do to others what you would have them do to you, for this sums up the Law and the Prophets"* (7:12 NIV).

Yes, God wants us to have joy in abundance, but how can we be brimming with happiness when we have slandered someone? The Lord tells us how to handle these situations. Jesus also instructs us in the book of Matthew: *"Then leave your gift before the altar, go to your brother, repent and forgive one another, be reconciled, and then return to the altar to offer your gift to God"* (5:24 THE VOICE).

The Lord is, indeed, beautiful the way He helps us to navigate this world with grace.

Sublime.

Dear Jesus, please help me to treat other people as I want them to treat me. Amen.

THE OFFSPRING OF GOD

It is the glory of God to conceal things,
but the glory of kings is to search things out.

 PROVERBS 25:2 ESV

Who can truly know the mind of God, for He is holy and perfect, and full of vast mystery?

The book of Acts says, *"Nor is he served by human hands, as though he needed anything, since he himself gives to all mankind life and breath and everything. And he made from one man every nation of mankind to live on all the face of the earth, having determined allotted periods and the boundaries of their dwelling place, that they should seek God, and perhaps feel their way toward him and find him. Yet he is actually not far from each one of us, for 'In him we live and move and have our being'; as even some of your own poets have said, 'For we are indeed his offspring'"* (17:25–28 ESV).

Heaven will be a time of wonderment, worship, fellowship, and all things glorious. It will be a time to get to know our God. What magnificent news. God is not fully known to us—nor would we ever want Him to be, since He is God!—but in Him we live and move and have our being. We are His offspring, and God is actually not far from each one of us.

The next time people try to steal our joy and our song, may we remember these words and meditate on them daily.

*Dear Lord, thank You for staying so close to me.
You are my joy, my song. I love You. Amen.*

GOD'S DREAMS
ARE BIGGER

*Listen carefully, those of you who make your plans
and say, "We are traveling to this city in the next few
days. We'll stay there for one year while our business
explodes and revenue is up." The reality is you have no
idea where your life will take you tomorrow. You are
like a mist that appears one moment and then vanishes
another. It would be best to say, "If it is the Lord's will
and we live long enough, we hope to do this project or
pursue that dream." But your current speech indicates
an arrogance that does not acknowledge the One who
controls the universe, and this kind of big talking is the
epitome of evil. So if you know the right way to live and
ignore it, it is sin—plain and simple.*

> JAMES 4:13–17 THE VOICE

People love making plans. Loads of them. College plans, marriage plans, career plans, vacation plans, and on and on. Goals are great, and plans are wonderful, but do we take them to our Lord to make sure He loves them too? Do we recognize that God has the final say—whether we give it to Him or not—in everything, including our plans?

How many times have our carefully calculated plans been disrupted, delayed, or destroyed? These interruptions can be a valuable spiritual reminder that we are not truly in control as we might think. So, for us to brazenly pronounce all that we *will* be doing, where we *will* be going, and how much money we *will* be making, well, that attitude doesn't please God. It is better to say, "If the Lord wills it." When we don't include God in our dreams or have a humble attitude about our tomorrows, is it because we think He is holding back on us? Jeremiah reminds us, *"For I know the plans I have for you, says the Lord. They are plans for good and not for evil, to give you a future and a hope"* (29:11 TLB).

Bottom line: God delights in giving us good gifts, and those include wonderful dreams and goals, a future and a hope! May we join Him in all we do, including the planning stages of our lives. After all, God's dreams are bigger and better than ours.

Lord, help my daily planner not to rule my life,
but for us to do life together. Amen.

A GENEROUS SPIRIT

Come [quickly] now, you rich [who lack true faith and hoard and misuse your resources], weep and howl over the miseries [the woes, the judgments] that are coming upon you. Your wealth has rotted and is ruined and your [fine] clothes have become moth-eaten. Your gold and silver are corroded, and their corrosion will be a witness against you and will consume your flesh like fire. You have stored up your treasure in the last days [when it will do you no good].

 JAMES 5:1-3 AMP

After reading the writings of James, we can safely say he does not hold back in trying to convince us that wealth can be mismanaged. And he is not talking about choosing the wrong stocks in the stock market! James is asking us whether we have such a gluttony for goods and a passion for possessions that we forget to have a passion for Christ. Do we put our faith in the material world? Are we so into getting more that the giving becomes forgotten along the journey?

But even people who have no money can be greedy about wealth. Obsession with money is as common as man—to want money if you don't have it and to want more money if you do have it. We can even become preoccupied with holding on to every penny instead of freely helping folks when we see the need. To be miserly is to know misery—not joy.

Giving is great, but what happens when we make a show of it? Jesus reminds us, *"Beware of practicing your righteousness before other people in order to be seen by them, for then you will have no reward from your Father who is in heaven. Thus, when you give to the needy, sound no trumpet before you, as the hypocrites do in the synagogues and in the streets, that they may be praised by others. Truly, I say to you, they have received their reward. But when you give to the needy, do not let your left hand know what your right hand is doing, so that your giving may be in secret. And your Father who sees in secret will reward you"* (Matthew 6:1–4 ESV).

Again, to have wealth is not evil—but rather, the adoration of it is. Do we instead glorify God with it? If so, then, let the joy begin!

Dear Lord, please give me a generous spirit. Amen.

ALL THINGS BEAUTIFUL

For the LORD grants wisdom!
From His mouth come knowledge
and understanding.

PROVERBS 2:6 NLT

The Bible has plenty to say on wisdom, and the Lord graciously gives it to us if we ask. While pondering the many facets of wisdom, one thought might be, *Our hearts yearn for beauty. Why is that?* After we create something beautiful—even if it doesn't have any immediate use—it, indeed, satisfies a need deep within us. God created all things good—all things beautiful. We are made in God's image, and so, when we create things of beauty, we are displaying and reflecting and celebrating that divine imprint on each of us. How splendid is that?

So, yes, our hearts desire beauty, and when that little garden we've been working on finally comes into full heavenly bloom, wow, it can give us a whole-body smile. To know and to thank the Source of all this gladness and glory and goodness, well, isn't that a bit of wisdom in itself? The book of Psalms says, *"The heavens are telling the glory of God; they are a marvelous display of His craftsmanship"* (19:1 ᴛʟʙ).

Yes, may we thank God more fervently for His majesty and beauty. May we thirst for His divine presence, and may we create alongside Him with pure joy!

Lord, what shall we create together today?
Thank You for all things beautiful! Amen.

TREASURES
IN HEAVEN

Behold, the wages of the laborers who mowed your
fields, which you kept back by fraud, are crying out
against you, and the cries of the harvesters have reached
the ears of the Lord of hosts. You have lived on the earth
in luxury and in self-indulgence. You have fattened your
hearts in a day of slaughter. You have condemned and
murdered the righteous person. He does not resist you.

JAMES 5:4-6 ESV

After reading this passage in James, we get the idea that some of the people of that time period had not embraced the joy of giving. James appears to be talking about people who cheated their workers and treated them horribly as they themselves lived a life of luxury. Even if our most selfish moments don't resemble this level of horror, there will always be room for improvement when it comes to sharing.

Even at a young age, people show signs of not wanting to share. Kids cling to their toys, their cheese sticks, and even those newly discovered dust balls off the floor. They want it all! And unfortunately, some of that attitude continues on into adulthood. But God gives us good gifts, and He expects us to share them. Our Lord tells us, *"Do not lay up for yourselves treasures on earth, where moth and rust destroy and where thieves break in and steal, but lay up for yourselves treasures in heaven, where neither moth nor rust destroys and where thieves do not break in and steal. For where your treasure is, there your heart will be also"* (Matthew 6:19–21 ESV).

But it is hard to let go of that old mindset. At some point God might discipline us if we refuse His guidance. But even then, there is hope and joy, for just as we correct our children because we love them, so God disciplines the ones He loves. And there is a joyful amen in that truth!

Dear God, even though I don't always enjoy Your divine rebukes, I thank You that You love me enough to guide me and correct me. In Jesus's powerful name I pray. Amen.

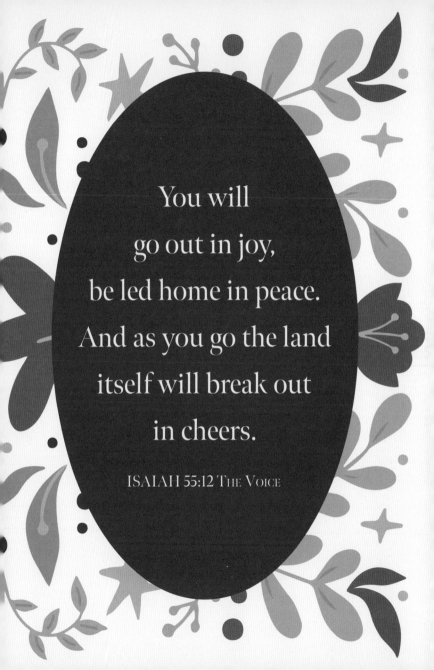

You will
go out in joy,
be led home in peace.
And as you go the land
itself will break out
in cheers.

ISAIAH 55:12 The Voice

DO NOT BE AFRAID

*Be patient, therefore, brothers, until the coming of the
Lord. See how the farmer waits for the precious fruit
of the earth, being patient about it, until it receives the
early and the late rains. You also, be patient. Establish
your hearts, for the coming of the Lord is at hand.*

JAMES 5:7-8 ESV

What is it like to suffer? No one escapes it,
so everyone will have their own unique and
painful stories.

In the previous verses, James was referring to the
anguish people endured at the hands of those who
took malicious advantage of them. At some point in our
lives, we all face people who are more than willing to
run roughshod over us, whether financially or otherwise.
When that happens, we typically moan and cry out for a
rescuer. Too many times mankind fails us, but God sees
all and offers hope. The Lord reminds of that assurance
in His holy Word.

In the book of Isaiah, the Lord tells us, *"Do not fear
[anything], for I am with you; do not be afraid, for I am*

your God. I will strengthen you, be assured I will help you; I will certainly take hold of you with My righteous right hand [a hand of justice, of power, of victory, of salvation]" (41:10 AMP).

God also tells us to be patient in suffering, which is not easy, but He promises to be with us always. He will never leave us nor forsake us.

James speaks of the farmer being patient, waiting for the early and late rains, and so we, too, must be patient as we wait for the Lord to come to our aid when times are oppressive here, and also as we wait for Christ's return, when all things will be made right in God's perfect judgment—when Christ will reign and Paradise will be regained!

Until then, no matter what we go through, God says not to fear, for He is with us. Yes, He will certainly take hold of us with His righteous right hand. And that, my friend, is joy divine.

Lord Jesus, help me to be patient in times of suffering.
Amen.

THE WAY OF GOD

Trust in the LORD with all your heart and lean not on your own understanding; in all your ways submit to Him, and He will make your paths straight.

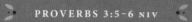

PROVERBS 3:5–6 NIV

This verse gives us some precepts that might make us uncomfortable. To trust in someone else, to submit to someone else, and to lean on someone else's understanding are all concepts that are alien to us. And yet this is the way of God.

The book of Isaiah gives us some insight on this topic: *"I don't think the way you think. The way you work isn't the way I work…. For as the sky soars high above earth, so the way I work surpasses the way you work, and the way I think is beyond the way you think. Just as rain and snow descend from the skies and don't go back until they've watered the earth, doing their work of making things grow and blossom, producing seed for farmers and food for the hungry, so will the words that come out of My mouth not come back empty-handed. They'll do the work I sent them to do,*

they'll complete the assignment I gave them" (55:8–11
THE MESSAGE).

God has proven Himself to be worthy of our trust, and His understanding is far beyond ours. Living life the Lord's way will never leave us empty-handed…

*Dear Jesus, help me always to listen to Your voice
and to submit to You in all things.
Thank You for making my paths straight. Amen.*

FREE OF
THE WHINE

Don't grumble about each other, brothers.
Are you yourselves above criticism? For see!
The great Judge is coming. He is almost here.
Let Him do whatever criticizing must be done.

JAMES 5:9 TLB

What do you normally find yourself grumbling about? Do you grumble when your food at the café arrives cold and you have to ask for a redo? Do you grumble at family members under your breath when they don't put the dishes up in the right place? Or maybe you grumble when you have to wait in a long line for your child to ride a pony at the festival? While most would probably grumble at these less than fortunate circumstances, a bigger problem surfaces when we start complaining about everything all the time.

God has never been big on grumbling, either, and for good reason. Unfortunately, at times the Israelites became notorious for it. The book of Psalms tells us, *"Then they despised the pleasant land; they did not* believe His promise. They grumbled in their tents and did not obey the LORD. So He swore to them with uplifted hand that He would make them fall in the wilderness" (106:24–26 NIV).

If we fill our lives with what is critical and cranky and crabby, how can we overflow with joy? All the endless nitpicking can elbow out the good stuff. And surely, we can see some things to sing about and praise the Lord for. So, if there is going to be a critical word here and there, leave it to God.

On our end, we can make a daily choice to be free of the whine and replace it with God and what is sublime!

Almighty God, please help me to stop grumbling over every little thing. I find fault with my friends, my family, my work, the weather, the food, well, almost everything! It is like I am on a treadmill of griping, and I can't get off. Forgive me. I need Your supernatural help to release me of this awful tendency. I want to so bask in Your radiant and holy presence that I forget to grumble! In Jesus's name I pray. Amen.

STAY THE COURSE!

Take the old prophets as your mentors. They put up
with anything, went through everything, and never
once quit, all the time honoring God. What a gift life
is to those who stay the course! You've heard, of course,
of Job's staying power, and you know how God brought
it all together for him at the end. That's because God
cares, cares right down to the last detail.

JAMES 5:10-11 THE MESSAGE

After reading this passage in James, it sort of makes us want to go off and hide. Or maybe it makes us want to do what James intended—stay the course.

You might be tempted to ask, "How in the world is that possible in such an impossible world?"

In Philippians, the apostle Paul, tells us, *"I'm not there yet, nor have I become perfect; but I am charging on to gain anything and everything the Anointed One, Jesus, has in store for me—and nothing will stand in my way because He has grabbed me and won't let me go. Brothers and sisters, as I said, I know I have not arrived; but there's one thing I am doing: I'm leaving my old life behind, putting everything on the line for this mission.*

I am sprinting toward the only goal that counts: to cross the line, to win the prize, and to hear God's call to resurrection life found exclusively in Jesus the Anointed" (3:12–14 THE VOICE).

Paul does not claim to be perfect, but he does know he has left his old life behind, and he's put everything on the line for his mission. Do these words describe our walk with Christ?

When we read the book of Job, we can see how he stayed the course. Even when everything went terribly wrong. Even when his wife encouraged him to do what was wrong. Even when his friends said the most appalling and discouraging things to him. Job stayed the course. God rewarded him mightily, and Job was never forgotten.

If all the world turns against us, will we stay the course, too? God is hoping we will say yes.

Lord, I am going to need Your supernatural strength to stay the course. Please help me every day, every hour. Amen.

FAITH, LOVE, PEACE

*The beginning of strife is like letting out water
[as from a small break in a dam; first it trickles and
then it gushes]; therefore abandon the quarrel before it
breaks out and tempers explode.*

PROVERBS 17:14 AMP

This verse in Proverbs is anything but simple to pull off, and yet it is the way of heaven. When you feel your temper rising, it is wise to take a few moments to calm down and allow God to defuse the situation before it explodes.

Second Timothy has something to say about this topic: *"Run away from childish indulgence. Run after mature righteousness—faith, love, peace—joining those who are in honest and serious prayer before God. Refuse to get involved in inane discussions; they always end up in fights. God's servant must not be argumentative, but a gentle listener and a teacher who keeps cool, working firmly but patiently with those who refuse to obey. You never know how or when God might sober them up with a change of heart and a turning* to the truth, enabling them to escape the Devil's trap, where they are caught and held captive, forced to run his errands" (2:22–26 THE MESSAGE).

What good advice! Can we do it? Not a chance. But with Christ, we can do all things.

Dear Lord, the next time I am tempted to let my temper get out of control, help me to keep my cool instead, rather than lashing out. Give me self-control and help me to become a good listener rather than a big talker. Amen.

EMBELLISHED WITH RELIGIOUS LACE

But above all, my brothers, do not swear,
either by heaven or by earth or by any other oath,
but let your "yes" be yes and your "no" be no,
so that you may not fall under condemnation.

JAMES 5:12 ESV

In a world filled with broken promises and empty words, the call to integrity is more important than ever. James, in his letter to the early Christian community, emphasized the significance of truthful speech and the power of our words. He reminds us that as followers of Christ, our words should carry weight, sincerity, and reliability. Our yes should mean yes, and our no should mean no.

Jesus, in the book of Matthew, also has something to say on the matter:

"And don't say anything you don't mean. This counsel is embedded deep in our traditions. You only make things worse when you lay down a smoke screen

of pious talk, saying, 'I'll pray for you,' and never doing it, or saying, 'God be with you,' and not meaning it. You don't make your words true by embellishing them with religious lace. In making your speech sound more religious, it becomes less true. Just say 'yes' and 'no.' When you manipulate words to get your own way, you go wrong." (5:33–37 THE MESSAGE).

How poignantly said! When we try and try to make our speech sound more religious, it comes off sounding less true. God does not want the people around us to think that our word is no more than noise or empty promises. God's Word is truth, and won't it be wonderful, indeed, when all the folks around us know we can be trusted to tell the truth?

Yes.

Father God, I want my words to count for something. When people hear me speak, may they automatically know that I am being truthful, because I have already proven myself to be a woman of integrity. May this be so. In Jesus's name I pray. Amen.

THE LOVELINESS OF SELF-CONTROL

Like a city that is broken down and without walls [leaving it unprotected] is a man who has no self-control over his spirit [and sets himself up for trouble].

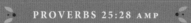

PROVERBS 25:28 AMP

In today's passage, we find a powerful analogy that compares a lack of self-control to a city without walls—a vulnerable and defenseless place. Just as walls protect a city from external threats, self-control acts as a fortress safeguarding our hearts, minds, and actions. Self-control is not merely about restraining ourselves from harmful or destructive behavior; it is about aligning our desires and actions with God's will. It's about growing in our godliness.

This passage in the book of Second Peter says it well: *"His divine power has granted to us all things that pertain to life and godliness, through the knowledge of him who called us to his own glory and excellence, by which he has granted to us his precious and very great promises, so that through them you may become partakers of the divine nature, having escaped from the corruption that is in the world because of sinful desire. For this very reason, make every effort to supplement your faith with virtue, and virtue with knowledge, and knowledge with self-control, and self-control with steadfastness, and steadfastness with godliness, and godliness with brotherly affection, and brotherly affection with love"* (1:3–7 ESV).

Yes, self-control can sound like a stifling restraint, but it is, in fact, the breeziest life, the loveliest life that could ever be lived. After all, God would only desire the best for us—for you.

Lord, with the power of Your Holy Spirit,
help me to live a godly life, which includes self-control.
Amen.

PRICELESS ADVICE

Is anyone among you suffering? Let him pray. Is anyone cheerful? Let him sing praise. Is anyone among you sick? Let him call for the elders of the church, and let them pray over him, anointing him with oil in the name of the Lord. And the prayer of faith will save the one who is sick, and the Lord will raise him up. And if he has committed sins, he will be forgiven.

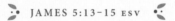

JAMES 5:13–15 ESV

There are so many kinds of prayers. Some beseech the Lord for mercy. Other times we might wrestle with the Almighty over an issue, or we might be listening for His still, small voice. Some prayers are lamenting over our sufferings, and other prayers might so reflect our happiness that we break out into songs of praise. If we are sick, James says we can call on the church leaders to anoint us with oil and pray over us in the name of the Lord. If we have committed sins, we can confess them to Christ, and He will be faithful to forgive us.

You might think, *Wow, that's a lot of talking to God.* But Christianity isn't a religion; it's a relationship with our Savior and Best Friend. First Thessalonians puts it simply: *"Pray without ceasing"* (5:17 ESV).

And in the book of Matthew, Jesus says, *"And when you pray, you must not be like the hypocrites. For they love to stand and pray in the synagogues and at the street corners, that they may be seen by others. Truly, I say to you, they have received their reward. But when you pray, go into your room and shut the door and pray to your Father who is in secret. And your Father who sees in secret will reward you. And when you pray, do not heap up empty phrases as the Gentiles do, for they think that they will be heard for their many words. Do not be like them, for your Father knows what you need before you ask him"* (6:5–8 ESV).

So, if you ever thought your prayers were too ordinary or too raw or too brief, you can be assured that God is not impressed with anything pompous, but He rewards those who come to Him with a humble heart.

Dearest Jesus, I love You. My heart is Yours. Amen.

PRAYER:
IT. CHANGES.
EVERYTHING.

*Therefore, confess your sins to one another and pray
for one another, that you may be healed. The prayer
of a righteous person has great power as it is working.
Elijah was a man with a nature like ours, and he prayed
fervently that it might not rain, and for three years
and six months it did not rain on the earth. Then he
prayed again, and heaven gave rain, and the earth
bore its fruit.*

JAMES 5:16–18 ESV

If you ever decide that you need some humility, well,
one sure way to gain some of it is to tell one of your
closest friends about your most shameful moments, and
then have her pray with you about them—right then.
Yep, that should do it. If you are truly honest about your
failings, it will surely melt that cocky arrogance right
out of you. Then she might get the idea she needs to
talk about her spiritual flaws too. Then more prayer. It
could turn into a serious prayer meeting. And a time

of healing. It could help change your life, her life—and perhaps some of the people who cross your paths. As James says, *"The prayer of a righteous person has great power as it is working"* (5:16 ESV).

The Bible has plenty more to say on prayer, so a deeper study would be meaningful. For instance, the book of Romans tells us, *"Meanwhile, the moment we get tired in the waiting, God's Spirit is right alongside helping us along. If we don't know how or what to pray, it doesn't matter. He does our praying in and for us, making prayer out of our wordless sighs, our aching groans. He knows us far better than we know ourselves, knows our pregnant condition, and keeps us present before God. That's why we can be so sure that every detail in our lives of love for God is worked into something good"* (8:26–28 THE MESSAGE).

Prayer: It. Changes. Everything.

Lord, may I pray in all the ways that please You. Thank You that You have sent Your Holy Spirit to help me to pray. May I be righteous before You, and may my prayers be effective. May I aspire to be like Elijah when I pray! Amen.

SHEPHERD'S HEART

*My dear friends, if you know people who have
wandered off from God's truth, don't write them off.
Go after them. Get them back and you will have
rescued precious lives from destruction and prevented
an epidemic of wandering away from God.*

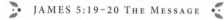

JAMES 5:19-20 THE MESSAGE

How exciting that we get to participate in the redemptive work of bringing wanderers back to the truth? We can help guide them back to God's love.

What a joy that through our words, prayers, and actions, we get to become vessels of God's redeeming and transformative power. The significance of this should not be underestimated. We get to participate in a divine rescue mission. We are tapping into God's sensitivity, compassion, and love for His children, and helping them find their way to forgiveness, healing, and restoration.

Jesus, in the book of Matthew, reminds us, *"If a man has a hundred sheep, and one of them has gone astray, does he not leave the ninety-nine on the mountains and go in search of the one that went astray? And if he finds it, truly, I say to you, he rejoices over it more than over the ninety-nine that never went astray. So it is not the will of my Father who is in heaven that one of these little ones should perish."* (18:12–14 ESV).

Yes, we are called to actively seek out those who are lost, extending a hand of compassion and guiding them back to the love and truth found in Jesus. The parable also reveals the joy that comes from restoration. When the shepherd finds the lost sheep, he rejoices more over that one sheep than over the ninety-nine that remained. May the relentless love of our Shepherd inspire us to reach out, and may we rejoice with heaven when wanderers are brought back in the embrace of God's love.

Dear Lord Jesus, thank You
for Your relentless love and pursuit of Your children.
Use me as Your instrument of grace, that I may have
the privilege of playing a part in bringing many sons
and daughters back to You. Amen.

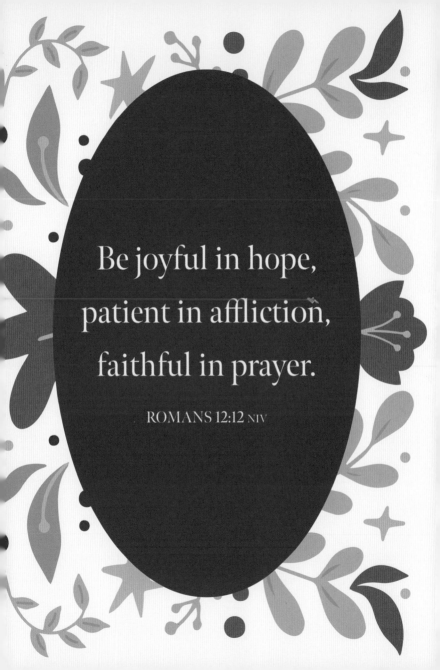

Be joyful in hope,
patient in affliction,
faithful in prayer.

ROMANS 12:12 NIV

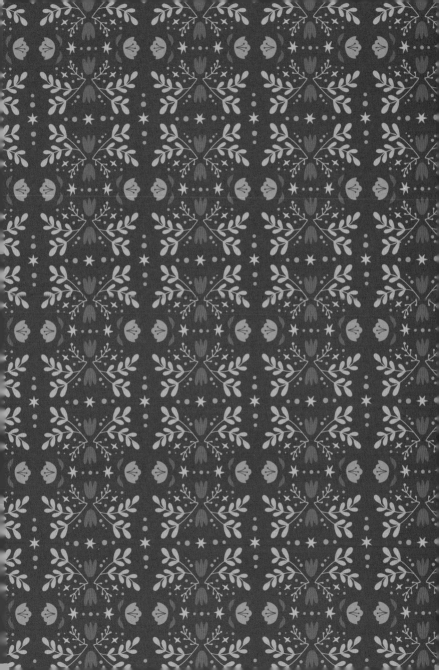

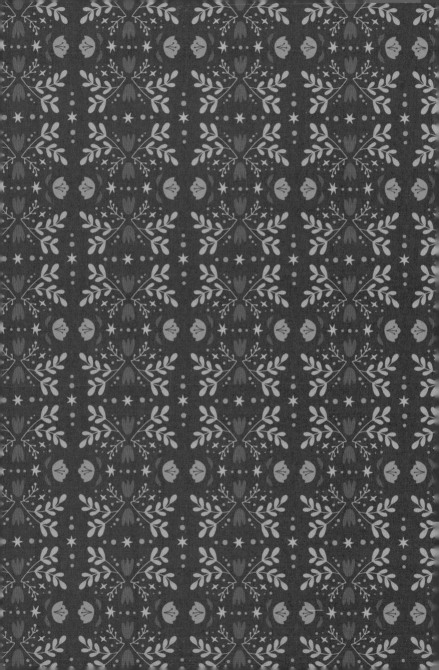